For more information visit our website
www.oup.co.uk/general/vsi/

Jo Labanyi

SPANISH LITERATURE

A Very Short Introduction

OXFORD
UNIVERSITY PRESS

OXFORD
UNIVERSITY PRESS

Great Clarendon Street, Oxford OX2 6DP
Oxford University Press is a department of the University of Oxford.
It furthers the University's objective of excellence in research, scholarship,
and education by publishing worldwide in

Oxford New York

Auckland Cape Town Dar es Salaam Hong Kong Karachi
Kuala Lumpur Madrid Melbourne Mexico City Nairobi
New Delhi Shanghai Taipei Toronto

With offices in

Argentina Austria Brazil Chile Czech Republic France Greece
Guatemala Hungary Italy Japan Poland Portugal Singapore
South Korea Switzerland Thailand Turkey Ukraine Vietnam

Oxford is a registered trade mark of Oxford University Press
in the UK and in certain other countries

Published in the United States
by Oxford University Press Inc., New York

© Jo Labanyi 2010

British Library Cataloguing in Publication Data

Data available

Library of Congress Cataloging in Publication Data

Data available

Typeset by SPI Publisher Services, Pondicherry, India
Printed in Great Britain by
Ashford Colour Press Ltd, Gosport, Hampshire

ISBN 978-0-19-920805-0

1 3 5 7 9 10 8 6 4 2

Contents

Acknowledgements

In writing this book, I have drawn on the work of many wonderful scholars. Since the format of the series precludes footnotes, I give a collective thank you here. Particularly useful critical texts in English are listed under Further reading. My special thanks go to two interlocutors whose conversation over the years has done much to shape my ideas: my colleague at New York University, Georgina Dopico-Black, whose suggestions for reading for the medieval and early modern periods made this book possible; and Elena Delgado, my co-author for a forthcoming project on the cultural history of modern Spanish literature. Xulia Santiso, director of the Casa-Museo Emilia Pardo Bazán in Corunna, and Rosa María Pereda, director of the Casa-Museo Benito Pérez Galdós in Las Palmas de Gran Canaria, went out of their way to provide me with material. Alberto Egea Fernández-Montesinos worked magic to get me access to Lorca's three house-museums in the course of one day. I thank María José Merlo Calvente for her individual tour of the Casa-Museo Federico García Lorca at the Huerta de San Vicente, and Leonardo Díaz Medina and José Pérez Rodríguez, director and guide of the Casa-Museo Federico García Lorca at Valderrubio, for devoting several hours to me; both visits were memorable. My thanks go also to Emma Marchant for her editorial guidance and to Julia Engelhardt for obtaining images and copyright clearance. I am especially indebted to the anonymous publisher's reader whose nuanced suggestions for medieval literature have made this a much better book.

List of illustrations

Introduction

This book aims to get beyond stereotypical assumptions about Spanish literature. To achieve that, I have organized my chapters thematically, focusing on current critical debates. While I have made a point of setting the writers discussed in their historical context, I have highlighted the aspects of their work likely to interest readers today. Whichever criteria one adopts in writing a literary history, some texts will be excluded; this book is no exception. This introduction identifies some frequent misconceptions about Spanish literature, in the process explaining why readers will not find in this book certain topics they may be expecting. The list of Further reading indicates sources that supplement my account. I have supposed no prior knowledge of Spanish literature or history, but have assumed that readers will be intellectually curious. If this book makes readers want to explore works by writers they did not know before, or think in new ways about writers previously encountered, it will have achieved its goal.

The first misconception I want to tackle concerns the literary figures of Don Quixote and Don Juan, likely to be known to most readers. Both have come to be seen, especially outside Spain, as tragic idealists bent on realizing an impossible dream – whether that of heroism in a prosaic world or self-realization through love. Such interpretations would baffle 17th-century Spaniards who read *Don Quixote* (*Don Quijote*, Part I: 1605, Part II: 1615) by Miguel de Cervantes (1547–1616) or saw the original Don Juan drama, *The Trickster of Seville* (*El burlador de Sevilla*, 1626), by Tirso de Molina (1584–1648). Nabokov, when preparing his 1951–2 Harvard *Lectures on Don Quixote*, was surprised, on going back to Cervantes' text, to find no trace of the idealist hero he was expecting but just a cruelly funny book. To set the record straight, I start by clarifying how the meanings of these literary figures have been transformed over time.

Cervantes unequivocally depicts Don Quixote as mad. At the end, he has him recant his madness in trying to live out in reality the novels of chivalry that have turned his head. The crazy knight immediately became a popular figure in court masques in Spain, England, and France, and in public festivities throughout the New World, as a butt of humour. Tirso's Don Juan is an example of how not to behave, whose sacrilege in defying God is stressed throughout. He is also guilty of flouting patriarchal authority, killing the father of one of his female victims – a high-ranking nobleman – whose statue drags him to hell. *The Trickster of Seville* is a play about blasphemy and disrespect for authority; Don Juan's persistent sexual violations are the means through which these themes are explored.

Both Don Quixote and Don Juan were reworked in 17th- and 18th-century European literature (and opera in Don Juan's case) as negative characters – though Mozart, associated with Enlightenment thinking, gives his Don Giovanni an individualist bravado. It was the Romantic period that turned both these heroes into tragic idealists. In Don Quixote's case, responsibility lies with the German Romantic theorists, the Schlegel brothers, who 'discovered' Spanish Golden Age (16th- and 17th-century) literature. The Schlegels praised Cervantes' novel, together with the drama of Pedro Calderón de la Barca (1600–81), for supposedly keeping alive the spirit of a heroic Middle Ages. This reading of *Don Quixote* has persisted outside (and sometimes inside) Spain

1. **Don Quixote as comic hero, doing penance in the Sierra Morena. Illustration by Gustave Doré to the 1863 French edition of** *Don Quixote*

until today. Don Juan entered the European Romantic imagination (Hoffmann, Pushkin, Byron) via Mozart's opera, not via Tirso's play. From the Romantic period, he came to be seen outside Spain as an expression of restless desire (as in Kierkegaard's seducer Johannes) whose blasphemous connotations, if present at all, take the form of a Faustian quest for knowledge.

Spanish Romantic writers took up Tirso's original blasphemer. The satanic hero of the narrative poem 'The Student of Salamanca' ('El estudiante de Salamanca', 1840), by José de Espronceda (1801–42), pursues the ghost of the lover he abandoned down to Hell, climaxing in a brilliant Gothic finale as he is embraced by her skeleton. The poem is an exaltation of man's refusal to bow to God's law. By contrast, the play *Don Juan Tenorio* (1844), by José Zorrilla (1817–93), defuses the revolutionary potential of Espronceda's rebel hero, having Doña Inés, the innocent convent girl he has abducted, return from the dead to save him through her undying love. In the final 'Apotheosis of Love', the two ascend to heaven on a cloud, confirming God's mercy. Zorrilla's play became institutionalized to the extent that it was performed throughout Spain every Halloween, because of its ghost scene, from the mid-19th to mid-20th centuries.

Don Quixote and Don Juan were read politically by early 20th-century Spanish writers, in the wake of Spain's 1898 war with the United States which cost Spain her last American and Asian colonies (Cuba, Puerto Rico, and the Philippines). Cervantes' hero was made into the emblem of a tragically defeated Spain by Miguel de Unamuno (1864–1936) and Azorín (1873–1967, pen-name of José Martínez Ruiz). But there is a twist, since his heroic idealism was seen by them as what Spain needed but lacked. This is not unlike Walter Benjamin's messianic concern with rescuing past utopian potential that was not allowed to prosper. Both Don Juan and Don Quixote were interpreted negatively by Ramiro de Maeztu (1874–1936) in a 1924 essay reflecting on the post-World War I crisis of humanism. For Maeztu, Don Juan represented the destructive egoism into which liberal modernity had degenerated, while Don Quixote embodied a hopelessly unpragmatic altruism. In a 1948 BBC radio play, the Republican exile in Britain Salvador de Madariaga (1886–1978) brought together six European versions of Don Juan to allegorize an aggressive Western individualism responsible for World War II. In 1952, Madariaga posited Don Juan as a symbol

2. The actress María Guerrero (1867–1928) as Doña Inés
in José Zorrilla's *Don Juan Tenorio*

of European imperialist expansion. In a different vein, Don Juan
had been taken up in 1935 by the Spanish avant-garde writer
and convert to fascism, Ernesto Giménez Caballero (1899–1988),
as the fascist superman who forces the (feminized) masses into
submission.

In his story 'Pierre Menard, author of the *Quixote*' ('Pierre Menard, autor del *Quijote*', 1939), Borges praised his character's brilliance in writing, in 1930s France, a text identical to that of Cervantes. It would indeed be extraordinary if later writers' interpretations of Don Quixote and Don Juan coincided with that of 17th-century Spaniards. This does not invalidate later readings (nor, of course, are they superior), but shows the importance of placing all readings in their historical context. We may note that Don Juan – often seen as the archetypal Spanish male – is idealized in the post-Romantic European imaginary but is treated critically by most Spanish (male) writers. That says something about a foreign tendency to idealize – literally 'romanticize' – Spanish culture.

The most frequent instance of this romanticizing tendency is the notion that Spanish culture is the expression of a tragic, primitive, folkloric Spain. Chapter 2 will explain how Spain came to be seen overseas, from the mid-17th century, as standing outside modernity. This misconception is graphically illustrated by the ways in which the poetry and plays of Federico García Lorca (1898–1936) have tended to be read abroad. Such readings evade recognition of Lorca's modernist aesthetics and of something else associated with the modern city: his homosexuality. The plays by Lorca discussed in this book are not his rural tragedies – by which he is almost exclusively known as a dramatist outside Spain – since these need no introduction. I merely note here that *Blood Wedding* (*Bodas de sangre*, 1933) and *Yerma* (1934) were staged in his day, under his supervision, with avant-garde sets; and that if he called *The House of Bernarda Alba* (*La casa de Bernarda Alba*, written 1936) a 'photographic document', this does not mean a naive realism but a succession of stylized black-and-white still images. The most striking 1930s Spanish documentary was Buñuel's surrealist film *Las Hurdes* (1933), which documented rural Spain through avant-garde montage, while Dalí had theorized documentary as avant-garde anti-art – Lorca had been close to both Buñuel and Dalí in the late 1920s.

3. Poster for the 1934 premiere of Federico García Lorca's play *Yerma*

This book also pays only brief attention to Lorca's *Gypsy Ballads* (*Romancero gitano*, 1928), by far his best-known book of poetry – something that exasperated him. If one compares Lorca's *Gypsy Ballads* with the popular ballad collections compiled by Spanish folklorists since the 1820s, it is clear that Lorca is not writing popular poetry but complex avant-garde works dense with highly sophisticated imagery. What Lorca takes from popular ballads is their dramatic conception and regular octosyllabic metre, the latter adopted as a disciplinary constraint. My discussion of works by Lorca that are less known outside Spain is intended to dispel the image of him as ingenuous Andalusian primitive, and to undo the tendency to back-project his tragic death – murdered on fascist orders early in the Spanish Civil War (18 August 1936) – onto his writing. Readers of this book will not find a tragic Spain of bullfights, blood, and death; there is plenty of that around elsewhere. Instead, my second chapter focuses on the relationship of Spanish literature to modernity.

Because I have wanted to counter the stereotype of a backward, rural Spain, I deal only briefly with Spain's folkloric ballad tradition, which has inspired both critics of democratic persuasion like Ramón Menéndez Pidal (mentioned in Chapter 2) and populist critics who have appealed to popular culture to keep the lower classes in their place. The Franco dictatorship's instrumentalization of folklore was a latter-day instance of the Herderian notion of literature as the expression of the national soul. This has been a salient feature of Spanish literary histories since their late 18th-century beginnings, coinciding with Herder: a notion of popular culture elaborated by urban intellectuals. I have focused in Chapter 4 on how this ballad tradition was reworked as Republican propaganda poetry during the Spanish Civil War.

This brings us to the most important choice I have made: to work against the national frame of reference that structures so many literary histories. In Spain, as elsewhere, literary history was consolidated as a discipline in the mid-19th century as part of the nation-formation process. The focus on texts that could be used for nation-building produced a skewed corpus, omitting much literature that was widely read, and giving the impression that literature's sole function was to 'write the nation'. A by-product was the exclusion or denigration of texts that smacked of foreign influence, privileging those seen as home-grown. This has aggravated the foreign tendency to suppose that Spanish culture is 'not fully European'. In this book, I have wanted to stress Spanish literature's multilingualism and, for much of its history, cultural diversity and cosmopolitanism: the focus of my first chapter.

Many literary histories have until recently given short shrift to women writers, for reasons that need no explaining. They have also tended to pay scant attention to gender and sexuality – so often the vehicles through which the 'national body' comes undone in literary texts. Yet so much literature is, and has always has been, concerned with love relationships. If my third chapter on gender and sexuality is the longest, it is because gender and sexuality are everywhere in literature; Spanish literature is no exception.

My short fourth chapter serves as a conclusion, picking up on issues of cultural ownership. The question of who has access to literature is important since, as the above discussion of Don Quixote and Don Juan shows, the meaning of literary texts is shaped by their readers. This book contributes to the process of giving meaning to Spanish literature not only through my own reading of it but also, in a more substantial way, by broadening access to it so that others can produce their own readings.

Chapter 1
Multilingualism and porous borders

This chapter considers how Spain's changing political and
linguistic map complicates attempts to define what is Spanish
about 'Spanish literature'. The question of how far back in time one
can take the term 'Spain' crystallized in the 1950s polemic between
two Spanish Republican exiles: Américo Castro and Claudio
Sánchez Albornoz. In *The Structure of Spanish History* (*España
en su historia*, 1948; revised as *La realidad histórica de España*,
1954), Castro argued that Spanish cultural identity was formed
from the creative if conflictive coexistence in medieval Iberia of
Christians, Muslims, and Jews. The Spanish nation created
through the 1469 dynastic union of the Crowns of Castile and
Aragon with the marriage of Isabella of Castile and Ferdinand of
Aragon (the 'Catholic Monarchs'), and clinched by their 1492
conquest of Granada (the last remaining Muslim kingdom in the
Iberian peninsula), ended this coexistence by expelling the Jews
(also in 1492) and reneging on the tolerance of Islam written into
Granada's capitulation treaty. Nonetheless, Castro argued that
the mental habits created by eight centuries of inter-faith
coexistence (since the 711 Muslim invasion) had become so
ingrained that they would leave an indelible mark. A defender of
the Christian basis of European civilization, Sánchez Albornoz
responded with his book *Spain, a Historical Enigma* (*España,
un enigma histórico*, 1956), arguing that the Spanish national
character (independent and democratic) was already latent in

the Celtiberian and Roman periods, and definitively formed under the (Christian) Visigoths. For Sánchez Albornoz, the eight centuries of Muslim rule in the peninsula, during which there was a strong Jewish cultural presence, were an anomalous hiccup which had left no trace on Spain's essential Christian destiny, resumed by the Catholic Monarchs as if nothing had happened. Both scholars can be criticized for their notion of an unchanging national identity but, if for Sánchez Albornoz it went back to the beginnings of time, for Castro it was at least formed through historical factors in the Middle Ages, even if he supposed that it remained fixed from 1492. In response to Sánchez Albornoz, Castro insisted that it was absurd to talk of 'Spanishness' before Spain existed as a nation; that is, before the Catholic Monarchs. For Castro, what exists in the Middle Ages is not 'Spain', although it would shape the Spanish nation that emerged from it, but a multiplicity of Christian and Muslim kingdoms, both of which had Jewish populations.

I start with this polemic since it illustrates the political stakes involved in use of the term 'Spain'. When referring to the medieval period, I have preferred the term 'Iberia'. This begs the question of whether the literature of medieval Iberia belongs in a history of 'Spanish literature'. I have included it in this book so as not to truncate, out of political correctness, the literature of those parts of the peninsula that would become Spain in the late 15th century. Although the term 'España' existed in the Middle Ages as a geographical label for the Iberian peninsula, to use the term 'Spain' before it existed as a political unit plays into nationalist agendas which this book wishes to avoid.

The multicultural Middle Ages: (i) The Muslim kingdoms

The term 'España' derives from Latin 'Hispania', the Roman Empire's name for its Iberian province. The Visigoths, the main Germanic tribe which invaded Hispania from the 3rd century CE, asserted nominal control over the peninsula by the late 6th century, with Toledo as their capital. Their language of writing was Latin. The 711 Muslim invasion was undertaken by a mix of Berbers and Arabs, who swept up through France till their advance was halted at Tours in 732. Retreating across the Pyrenees, they held most of the Iberian peninsula, ruled by the Caliphate of Damascus, apart from an initially tiny Christian enclave in Asturias and, from 759, the north-eastern Hispanic Marches under Frankish control. In 756, Abd-ar-Rahman I, a refugee from the overthrown Umayyad dynasty in Damascus, set up the independent Emirate (subsequently Caliphate) of Cordoba, centralizing power in al-Andalus (the Arabic term for Muslim Iberia). The highpoint of Andalusi cultural splendour (I use this term to avoid confusion with modern 'Andalusian') was the 10th century, after which increasing intolerance set in, with the Cordoban Caliphate splintering in 1031 into numerous city-states (*taifas*). It was, however, during the *taifa* period that Andalusi poetry reached its height. By 1000, the emerging Christian kingdoms of León, Castile, Navarre, and Catalonia (the latter independent from French control since 989) controlled roughly the top third of the peninsula. The major political shift came with Castile's 1085 conquest of Toledo, a symbolic prize as the former capital of a Christian Visigothic Iberia, establishing Castile as the leading Christian kingdom. Portugal became independent in 1139. The Kingdom of Aragon, which split from Navarre in 1043, emerged as a major player when in 1137 it united with Catalonia to form the Crown of Aragon. By 1238, Aragon had conquered Muslim Majorca and Valencia. The Kingdoms of Castile and León merged definitively in 1217 as the Crown of Castile, which by 1248 had conquered the former Muslim kingdoms of Cordoba, Murcia, Jaén, and Seville. From this point, al-Andalus was reduced to the Kingdom of Granada (covering modern Almería, Granada, and Málaga) until its fall to the Crown of Castile in 1492 – the *annus mirabilis* that also saw Columbus's discovery of America under Castilian Crown patronage.

In al-Andalus, until 1085 covering most of the peninsula, the language of state and culture was pan-Islamic formal Arabic, with a vernacular dialect of Arabic being spoken, and a range of intermediate registers being used as circumstance required. The Berbers, who formed the majority of the 711 invaders, and who instituted the Almoravid and Almohad dynasties of the 11th to 13th centuries, were partly Arabized. The conquered population shifted from Andalusi Romance ('Romance' being the term for the family of European languages that developed from Latin) to Arabic as they progressively converted to Islam (around 80% of the population by 1100). The Islamic *dhimma* tradition regulating non-Muslim minorities granted Christian and Jewish communities protection, respecting their religious and linguistic practices, in return for certain obligations, including taxes. The Christian minority (Mozarabs) spoke Romance and vernacular Arabic, and wrote in Latin (at first) and a simplified version of formal Arabic (Middle Arabic). From the late 9th to the mid-11th centuries, biblical texts were intensively translated into Arabic since the Mozarabs were 'losing' Latin. The Jewish minority spoke Romance (Jews arrived in Roman Hispania c. 300 CE) or increasingly, thanks to the many Jews who came to al-Andalus from the Middle East and North Africa, Arabic. They normally wrote in Middle Arabic, rendered in Hebrew script when communicating among themselves since Hebrew (not a spoken language) was the prestige language of their religious practices, as formal Arabic was for Muslims. Thus non-Muslims routinely moved across languages, whether in speech or writing or both; and diglossia between spoken and written languages was standard for the whole population.

I cannot discuss here the major corpus of Andalusi Arabic philosophy – by writers such as Averroes (Ibn Rushd) or the Arabic-language Jewish writer Maimonides (Rabbi Moshe ben Maimon), both 12th century – except to note its importance for reconnecting Europe with Greek philosophical and scientific writings lost in the original but conserved in Arabic translation.

The literature of Muslim Iberia, whether written in Arabic or Hebrew, is seldom included in histories of Spanish literature. Indeed, while the inhabitants of the Christian kingdoms are often anachronistically called 'Spaniards', the inhabitants of al-Andalus are traditionally referred to as 'Moors'. This is obviously discriminatory. Most scholars of Spanish literature do not know Arabic or Hebrew. By contrast, al-Andalus retains a huge symbolic value for Islamic and Jewish cultures – apart from al-Qaeda's rhetoric, historical dramas set in al-Andalus are broadcast on Arabic-language satellite television, while Jewish studies call the 11th century in Sepharad (the Hebrew name for Iberia) the 'Golden Age of Hebrew poetry'.

How, then, do we classify the Arabic love poetry of al-Andalus? This first example has European implications since Arabic scholars and many Romance Studies scholars regard it as a source of 12th-century Occitan (formerly known as Provençal) courtly love poetry – the earliest known literary corpus in a Romance language, whose idealization of love has been seen as the origin of a specifically European sensibility. There was considerable cultural contact between Aquitaine and al-Andalus. In 1064, a large contingent of Muslim singing girls was taken to Aquitaine as military booty from Aragon (much of it under Muslim rule till 1118) by William VIII of Aquitaine, father of the first troubadour (William IX). Well-known Occitan troubadours visited the Christian courts of Barcelona, Aragon, and Castile, where Arabic culture retained its prestige. The Arabic-origins thesis for Occitan lyric was widely accepted until Napoleon's conquest of Egypt produced a colonial construction of Arabic culture as inferior; an argument that emerged at this time was that a poetry that exalted women could not have come from Muslims. The outstanding Andalusi love poet was Ibn Zaydun (1003–70), a product of the Cordoban Umayyad Caliphate's cultural flowering, who retained his prestige after the Caliphate's collapse in 1031. His best-known poems are dedicated to the penultimate Umayyad Caliph's daughter, who hosted the most refined literary salon in Cordoba.

The Cordoban prose writer Ibn Hazm (994–1064) has fared better with Hispanists, thanks to the 1952 Spanish translation of his love treatise *The Dove's Neck-Ring*, with a famous prologue by the philosopher Ortega y Gasset (1883–1955). Ibn Hazm's polemical religious writings show his familiarity with Hebrew and Christian scriptures. He died in exile, after the Umayyads' fall, in the Muslim *taifa* of Majorca. Border crossing (geographic and cultural) is a feature of many Andalusi writers. Ibn Quzman (1078–1160) – noted for his poetic mix of formal and vernacular Arabic, incorporating Romance elements, in songs that celebrate wine, women, and song – sought patronage throughout the *taifa* kingdoms. The Murcia-born Sufi mystic Ibn 'Arabi (1165–1240) traversed al-Andalus and the Maghreb, in 1201 leaving for Mecca, Palestine, Syria, Iraq, and Anatolia in search of fellow Sufi scholars, living his last fourteen years in Damascus, where his domed shrine exists today.

Jewish poets too crossed multiple borders. The Granada-born Moses Ibn Ezra (c. 1055 to after 1138), the best-known Arabized poet of the Hebrew Golden Age, fled to the Christian north, like many other Jews, after the 1090 Almoravid invasion which ended the previous religious tolerance. He found Christian Iberia culturally barren, though it had not yet become intolerant of religious minorities. In addition to his secular and religious poetry in Hebrew, he is known for his prose works in Arabic, including an invaluable treatise on Andalusi Hebrew poetry. Judah Halevi (c. 1075–1141), the most celebrated poet of his age, followed an inverse trajectory. Born in Tudela (Navarre), then under Muslim rule, he established himself in Toledo around 1100, fifteen years after its capture by Alfonso VI of Castile, where he worked with Alfonso's Jewish court physician, also travelling widely around al-Andalus. His large poetic corpus in Hebrew includes secular verse, adapting the forms and content of Arabic poetry to Hebrew, and sacred verse, which became incorporated into the Jewish liturgy. In 1140, he renounced this acculturation and left for Jerusalem, apparently not getting beyond Egypt, where he tried (unsuccessfully) to purge his poetry of its Arabic elements.

One cannot simply appropriate these writers for 'Spanish literature', ignoring their position within the Arabic and Hebrew literary canons. But, given the stress in contemporary postcolonial studies on the possibility, if not desirability, of double cultural allegiance, surely they should be seen as 'Spanish' as well as Arabic or Hebrew, giving full recognition to the border crossings – between languages, between Andalusi city-states, between Muslim and Christian Iberia, between Iberia and North Africa or the Middle East – that mark most of their careers. This multiculturalism is embodied in a popular lyric genre to which Judah Halevi was a major contributor: the *muwashshah* – the one Andalusi genre which has been enthusiastically claimed by Spanish scholars. Written in Arabic or Hebrew, the *muwashshah*, dating from the 11th century and anthologized from the 12th, is characterized by a final strophe (*kharja*) quoting another song (probably determining the whole poem's rhyme). About one-third of the *kharjas* (in poems devoted to panegyric) are in formal Arabic; of the rest (in poems devoted to love and wine), most are in vernacular Arabic, but around 10% are in Andalusi Romance, written in Arabic script. When this was discovered in 1948, Spanish scholars were ecstatic at what they claimed was poetry in a Romance vernacular that predated the Occitan lyric. It became frequent to discuss the Romance *kharjas* without reference to the Arabic or Hebrew *muwashshah* of which they are part, as if this were purely 'Spanish' poetry. In fact, the Romance *kharjas*, apart from being tiny in number (the entire *kharja* corpus contains only 400 Romance words), mix Romance with colloquial Arabic. The same poets wrote *muwashshah* with *kharjas* in Arabic and in Romance. The *muwashshah* should clearly be studied as part of 'Spanish literature', but with an appreciation of the genre's penchant for bilingualism and the dialogic counterpoint of formal and colloquial registers. Some include gender-switching:

20% of vernacular Arabic *kharjas* and 75% of Romance *kharjas* are female-voiced, though male-authored.

The volume devoted to al-Andalus in the *Cambridge History of Arabic Literature* sets an example by including Ramon Llull (1232–1315), revered as founding father of Catalan literature, on the grounds of Arabic influence on his work and his claim to have first written in Arabic his monumental *Book of Contemplation* (*Libre de contemplació*). Born in Majorca three years after its capture from Muslim rule, he immersed himself in Arabic scholarship, developing a project for universal conversion to Christianity via intercultural debate. His *Book of the Gentile and the Three Wise Men* (*Libre del gentil e los tres savis*), based on an Arabic source, sets out the common ground between the three Abrahamic faiths. His mystical work, *The Book of the Lover and the Beloved* (*Libre d'amic e amat*), contained in his novel *Blanquerna*, explicitly imitates Arabic Sufi texts. Another Majorcan, the Franciscan friar Anselm Turmeda (1355?–1430?), moved to Tunis around 1387, converting to Islam (as Abdallah al-Tarjuman), and writing a refutation of Christianity in Arabic while simultaneously composing texts in Catalan.

The multicultural Middle Ages: (ii) The Christian kingdoms

Llull's example shows that, in medieval Spain, multiculturalism was not restricted to Muslim territories. The hero of what would become constructed as Spain's foundational epic, *Poem of the Cid* (*Poema de mio Cid*, see Chapter 2), fought for Muslim as well as Christian masters; his name derives from the Arabic *Sidi* ('my Lord').

There is ongoing debate about the extent of the intercultural dialogue – known in Spanish as *convivencia* – between Christians, Muslims, and Jews in Christian Iberia, with recent scholarship suggesting that coexistence was made possible by periodic ritual violence against minorities. There is, however, agreement that

4. Still from the animated film *The Cid, the Legend* (*El Cid, la leyenda*) (directed by José Pozo, 2003)

continuous fighting between Christian and Muslim kingdoms, and a general lack of social assimilation (as in Muslim Iberia), coexisted with a high level of cultural hybridity. Hostility to Islam did not mean lack of appreciation of Arabic culture, much of which was secular. Arabic remained the language of cultural prestige in areas where Islam had been defeated. The Christian kingdoms, much like their Muslim counterparts, offered guarantees to Muslim and Jewish communities in return for paying taxes and observing certain restrictions. Regulations on clothing were often unenforced; indeed, there are cases of Christian kings and bishops being buried in Moorish finery. Moorish architectural styles – known when adopted in Christian territory as Mudejar, the term for Muslims under Christian rule – were promoted by Christian patrons, remaining the norm for prestigious buildings, including Christian churches and Jewish synagogues, long after conquest. A key example of this cultural hybridity is Toledo, following its capture by Alfonso VI of Castile in 1085; in addition to its many examples of Mudejar architecture, it would become a major centre of translation.

In early medieval Christian Iberia, Latin was the language of writing, with the different areas speaking varieties of Ibero-Romance.

Basque (*euskara*), a non-Indo-European language predating the Roman conquest, was (and is) the vernacular on both sides of the west-coast border with France. Of these Ibero-Romance vernaculars, the most important were Galician-Portuguese, Asturian, Leonese, Castilian, Aragonese, Catalan, and the dialects of Catalan spoken in Valencia and the Balearic Islands. They were assumed to be spoken versions of Latin till the late 11th century, when the newly introduced Carolingian reforms instituted a phonetic pronunciation of Latin, clearly distinct from the Romance vernaculars. The first texts written in Romance appear shortly after, with Latin remaining the standard literary language till the mid-13th century and continuing alongside Romance long after that. We should not forget the body of medieval Latin writing produced in Christian Iberia, whose cosmopolitanism fits ill with nationalist conceptions of literary history. Jews in Christian territory spoke the Romance vernacular, writing in Latin or Hebrew – or, in the case of those who fled north from Almoravid or subsequent Almohad intolerance, in Arabic. Those members of the population, of whatever faith, who had spoken or written Arabic before Christian conquest continued to do so, though with increasing acculturation to the Romance vernacular.

It was in this context of linguistic diversity that, in the early 12th century, Toledo translators embarked on translating into Latin the massive corpus of Arabic texts, many from the Middle East, in Toledo's libraries. While the aim was to make available Arabic scholarship, a result was the discovery by European scholars of previously unknown Greek philosophical and scientific writings which had been translated in Baghdad. Scholars from all over Europe converged on Toledo at this time, including the English Robert of Ketton commissioned by the French Abbot of Cluny to translate the Koran into Latin. Translations were undertaken collaboratively by teams of Mozarabs (Christians who had lived under Muslim rule), Mudejars (Muslims who stayed after Christian conquest), and Jews (fluent in Arabic). Some of these Mozarabs and Jews were recent arrivals in Toledo, fleeing persecution by the Almoravids or, from 1140, the more intolerant

Almohads who succeeded them in al-Andalus. The decisive shift in this translation enterprise took place in the 13th century with Alfonso X of Castile's decision to sponsor the translation of Toledo's Arabic scholarship into the local Romance vernacular: Castilian. Despite – or because of – the reverence accorded Arabic as the language of science and culture, this was a colonial project designed to grant Castilian the status of an imperial language, equal to Arabic or Latin. This is the start of the process that would convert Castilian into 'Spanish'.

Alfonso X, known as 'the Wise' (1221–84, ruled 1252–84), was a polymath educated to be a prince by his father Ferdinand III (responsible for conquering Cordoba, Murcia, Jaén, and Seville in the mid-13th century) through immersion in the Arabic *belles-lettres* tradition of manuals for the art of living. Ferdinand compiled for him an anthology of Arabic wisdom literature translated into Castilian. This was the first time that an interest had been taken in Arabic literary (as opposed to philosophical and scientific) texts – an interest that Alfonso, familiar with Arabic, would make his own. Alfonso's commission of a Castilian translation of the Arabic framed-tales *Calila and Dimna* (*Calila e Dimna*, c. 1251), itself translated from the Persian, shows his understanding of culture as a translation process. This Persian-derived tradition of stories within stories – as in the *Thousand and One Nights* – generated various Castilian offspring, including the wisdom text *Count Lucanor* (*Conde Lucanor*, 1335) composed by Alfonso's nephew, Don Juan Manuel (1282–1348).

The translations from Arabic to Castilian commissioned by Alfonso X include histories, books of chess, manuals of practical philosophy, and works of astrology, astronomy, and geology. In addition, he supervised the composition in Castilian of legal codifications such as the *Seven-Part Code* (*Siete Partidas*), a history of Spain (*Estoria de Espanna*) and of the world (*General Estoria*), and, in Galician-Portuguese, *Songs to the Virgin Mary* (*Cantigas de Santa Maria*). Galician-Portuguese was the language of lyric

5. Group of troubadours from Alfonso X's, *Songs to the Virgin Mary* (*Cantigas de Santa Maria*)

poetry throughout western and central Iberia from the late 12th to the mid-to-late 14th centuries: an originally oral genre that during this period became recorded in songbooks. In eastern Iberia, the language of lyric poetry was Occitan, increasingly Catalanized in the 14th to 15th centuries. When Castilian became a standard language of lyric poetry in the 15th century (the first recorded examples are mid-14th century), it frequently appeared in courtly songbooks (*cancioneros*) alongside lyrics in Catalan and Italian, thanks to Aragon's Italian possessions (see below).

Medieval literature in Castilian routinely draws on Arabic, Latin, and/or French literary traditions. Prior to the concept of the original author, no distinction was drawn between original composition and translation: literary and historical works integrate earlier texts, from multiple languages and genres, into their fabric. The multiculturalism of medieval literature must be stressed: the nation-state, in its modern sense of a political unit based on one race, one language, and one culture, did not yet exist. This trans-European and trans-Mediterranean imagination is seen still in the late 15th- and early 16th-century novels of chivalry, whose popularity – enhanced through the printing press in the 16th century, when their readers included the young St Teresa of Avila, St Ignatius of Loyola, and Charles V – led to their mocking in *Don Quixote*. The most widely read were the Catalan-Valencian *Tirant lo Blanc* (1490) – mostly written by Joannot Martorell (1413–68) and completed by Martí Joan de Galba (?–1490) – and the Castilian *Amadis of Gaul* (*Amadís de Gaula*, oldest known printing 1508), by Garci Rodríguez de Montalvo (?–1504). Both acknowledge their incorporation of prior Arthurian material: *Tirant* starts by adapting the early 13th-century Anglo-Norman chivalric romance *Guy of Warwick* (*Gui de Warewic*); Rodríguez de Montalvo states that the first three books of his *Amadís* are compiled from a 14th-century version (lost but known to have existed). Their characters, none of them Spanish, wander between the poles of England and Constantinople. Spanish literary texts from the 15th to 17th centuries remind us that the interface with Islam remained an everyday reality in the early modern period, through ongoing contact with the Ottoman Empire in the Mediterranean.

Political unification and cultural homogenization

This cultural diversity takes a brutal knock with the beginnings in 1492 of a process of national unification that would be clinched politically in the early 18th century and culturally in the late 19th century. The common attribution of national unification to the Catholic Monarchs overlooks the process's cumulative nature. Isabella and Ferdinand ruled their kingdoms separately on acceding to their respective thrones in 1474 and 1479. Although their grandson Charles V inherited the thrones of both Castile and Aragon in 1516, Aragon retained its separate legal and administrative system till 1716. What the Catholic Monarchs secured in 1492, through conquest of the last Iberian Muslim Kingdom of Granada and expulsion of the Jews, was religious unity – up to a point, for, as we shall see, enforced conversion of Muslims was not imposed across the national territory till 1528, under Charles V, and the Moriscos (Muslims who stayed after 1492) were finally expelled in 1609–14, under Philip III. In the New World, however, the indigenous population was subjected to enforced conversion from the moment of conquest. Isabella's patronage of Columbus brought the Americas under Castilian rule – a decisive factor in the parallel process of linguistic homogenization whereby Castilian became established as 'Spanish'. In the same year, 1492, Antonio de Nebrija's first grammar of the Castilian language (*Gramática de la lengua castellana*) insisted that language was 'the companion of empire'; Castilian, in other words, was the new Latin.

This religious homogenization process had profound implications for cultural practices. The institution responsible for enforcing it – at home and in the Americas – was the Inquisition, created in 1478 to deal with Christianized Jews (*conversos*) suspected of lapsing into Judaism. The 1492 expulsion decree made conversion obligatory for those Jews who chose to stay (many had already converted after the widespread pogroms that began in 1391). By 1502, the initial tolerance of Islam in conquered Granada had given way to a Castilian policy of enforced conversion, extended in 1528 to the Crown of Aragon (Valencia had an especially significant Morisco population). This cultural repression, enhancing the sacred status of Arabic calligraphy at a time when education in Castilian was the only option, paradoxically increased the Moriscos' production – dating back to the late 14th century – of *aljamiado* texts, written in Castilian using Arabic script. In 1567, all Muslim practices, including clothing, song, dance, and use of the Arabic language, were banned. The result was the 1568–71 Alpujarras Revolt in Granada province. The savage reprisals led to the Granadan Moriscos' forced dispersal throughout Castile, and in 1609–14 to the expulsion of all Moriscos from Spain, despite the fact that, several generations after conversion, many had become sincere Christians. Chapter 2 will discuss the persistence of this ethnic diversity in Spain's early modern literature, despite the state's attempts to eliminate it.

The impact of linguistic homogenization on the Romance vernaculars was also drastic. Galician-Portuguese continued to be used for lyric poetry throughout Castile till the 16th century, alongside Castilian. Otherwise, the Galician language became marginalized, particularly after Portugal split off as an independent kingdom in 1139, with Galicia (part of the Kingdom of León) coming under Castilian control from 1217. Basque (*euskara*) was used in popular poetry but produced few written literary texts before the late 19th century. Although the post-1492 Spanish nation comprised the Crowns of Castile and Aragon, the court resided in Castile, privileging use of Castilian. Aragonese, having no literary tradition, declined. Catalan, however, had a rich literary heritage, shaped by its trans-Mediterranean role, placing it at the interface between Christianity and Islam (as evidenced in Llull's work), and by its links with Occitan culture, maintained till the 13th century. Troubadour poetry in Occitan was encouraged at the Catalan court by the poet-kings Alfons I (1162–96) and Pere I (1196–1213). This lyric tradition was developed by the Valencian Ausiàs March (1397–1459), the first major poet to write in Catalan following Ramon Llull's establishment of Catalan's credentials as the language of serious prose works. Catalan was the administrative language of the Crown of Aragon's Mediterranean sea-borne empire, ruled from Barcelona, which at one point stretched from south-west France to Greece. Like medieval Catalan literature, Aragon's empire peaked in the 14th and 15th centuries. After that, the prestige of Castilian as the language used at court produced a language shift as Catalan writers increasingly switched to Castilian.

This internal homogenization process was, however, accompanied by significant cultural contact in Europe. Aragon's possessions in Naples, Sicily, and Sardinia remained in Spanish hands till the 1713 Treaty of Utrecht, ending the War of the Spanish Succession. Spain reconquered Naples and Sicily in 1734, from when they were ruled as a joint kingdom, independent of the Spanish Crown but dynastically linked to it, until liberated by Garibaldi in the mid-19th century. King Charles III of Spain (ruled 1759–88) was formerly King of Naples and Sicily. This Italian connection is visible in many Spanish literary works, whose characters (including Don Juan) spend time in Italy, as did a number of Spanish writers (including Cervantes). This contact facilitated the introduction of Italian humanist ideas into Spain from the early 15th century, establishing Petrarchism and Neoplatonism as the dominant literary love discourses, and also producing a resurgence of writing in Latin. The initial conduits for the transmission of Italian humanism were Catalonia and Valencia. Valencia became a major literary centre in the 15th century, contributing to the formation of Castilian Renaissance culture. The latter was consolidated in the early 16th century, its major figure being the soldier-poet Garcilaso de la Vega (1501–36) who served in Charles V's army in Italy, France, and Germany. Spain's 16th-century wars against France (mostly in Italy) and England (at sea) meant that Spanish literature was widely read in both countries, in the original and in translation. Philip II was, of course, briefly King-Consort of England while married to Mary Tudor (1554–8). Despite limitations on study abroad from the mid-16th century, thousands of Spaniards circulated through Europe in the Habsburg war machine, with the Europe-wide wars of Charles V as Holy Roman Emperor (doubling with his role as Charles I of Spain 1516–56) and the ongoing wars against Protestantism in the Low Countries (inherited by the future Charles V in 1506 and passing to his Spanish Habsburg successors). The historian John

Elliott has noted that early modern Spaniards had a wider experience of the world than the members of any other European nation.

This cultural contact in Europe came to an end with the 1648 Treaty of Westphalia, which divested Spain of the remainder of the Low Countries (it had lost what became the Dutch Republic in 1581), leaving it limited territorially in Europe to its present boundaries in the Iberian peninsula. The next stage of the story is the consolidation of political and cultural homogenization at home. The new centralizing Bourbon monarchy punished the Crown of Aragon (comprising Aragon, Catalonia, Valencia, and the Balearic Islands) for having supported the losing Habsburg side in the War of the Spanish Succession, through the 1707–16 Nueva Planta decrees which abolished the Crown of Aragon, suppressing its local customary laws (*fueros*). Only from this date can we talk of Spain's administrative unification. In 1768, the modernizing Bourbon monarch Charles III decreed Castilian the obligatory language of administration and education throughout the national territory, enforcing linguistic unification at the level of official usage. The Basque Country and Navarre kept their *fueros* till 1876, when the Carlists (supporters of a conservative pretender to the throne, representing the Catholic feudal oligarchy in the Basque Country, Navarre, and parts of the former Crown of Aragon) were definitively defeated in the last of three civil wars fought since the 1830s against the centralizing liberal state. What, however, clinched the conversion of the country's inhabitants into national citizens was the creation from the 1830s of a national Castilian-language press, plus the 1857 introduction of a state education system. The secondary-school curriculum included national (meaning Castilian) literature. The mid-19th century sees the systematic production of histories of Spain and of Spanish literature, mostly by authors supportive of the liberal state's centralizing agenda. As noted in the Introduction, the canon of Spanish literature established by this process is skewed accordingly, with cultural diversity edited out.

These mid-19th-century cultural developments explain why Spain's loss of most of its Spanish American possessions between 1810 and 1824 made little public impact, for the empire was seen as belonging to the Crown rather than the nation. By contrast, when Spain lost Cuba, Puerto Rico, and the Philippines in 1898, this was perceived as a national disaster, affecting all citizens. It is only from the late 19th century that one can really talk of Spain as a nation-state in the full modern sense of the term: that is, as a national collective whose members feel a sense of shared values (though many resented this imposition). The Spanish Royal Academy dictionary first gives the term '*nación*' its modern sense of 'nation-state' (as opposed to its earlier sense of 'ethnic group') in 1884. Although the notion that a nation's literature is the expression of its people (the *Volk*) dates back to the Romantic period, it is from the late 19th century that one can talk of 'Spanish literature' as an established corpus – one that remains largely intact today, apart from the recent addition of some women writers and the development of separate canons for Spain's 'historic nationalities': Catalonia, Galicia, and the Basque Country.

The rise of non-state nationalisms

The triumph of the nation-state in late 19th-century Europe coincided with the emergence of non-state nationalisms, putting multilingualism back on the agenda less than a century after Charles III's enforced Castilianization. Nationalist movements emerged in Catalonia, Galicia, and the Basque Country from the mid-19th century. Catalan and Galician nationalism were initially based on demands for recognition of a separate linguistic and cultural rather than political identity. Literature played a major role in this process.

Catalan nationalism, partly reacting against massive industrialization in the mid-19th century, looked back to the impressive medieval Catalan literary tradition. The 1859 institution of the Jocs Florals (reviving Catalan medieval poetic contests) was imitated in Galicia and the Basque Country in 1861 and 1879. Catalan had remained a spoken language among the bourgeoisie, and the revival (*Renaixença*) of Catalan literary production dates back to the poem 'Ode to the Fatherland' ('Oda a la pàtria', 1833) of the banker Buenaventura Carles Aribau (1798–1862). Key writers of the *Renaixença* were Jacint Verdaguer (1835–1902), known for his epic poems, particularly *Canigó* (1885) which narrates Catalonia's legendary origins; the realist novelist Narcís Oller (1846–1930, see Chapter 2); and the dramatist Àngel Guimerà (1845–1924), whose play *Lowlands* (*Terra baixa*, 1897) was filmed by Leni Riefenstal (*Tiefland*, 1954) among others. The work of Verdaguer and Guimerà has a strong Romantic, telluric streak. Catalan literary production continued to grow with the *fin-de-siècle* Modernist movement (*modernisme*), corresponding to the contemporary pan-European cultural trends of Symbolism and Art Nouveau. *Modernisme* sought to renovate Catalan culture through a productive dialogue with Europe: for example, the poet Joan Maragall (1880–1911). In the early 20th century, with Catalan nationalist politics dominated by the bourgeois Regionalist League (Lliga Regionalista), a classicizing tendency, *noucentisme*, emerged, embodied by the protagonist Teresa of the novel *La ben plantada* (1911, rough translation *The Solidly Rooted Girl*) by Eugeni d'Ors (1881–1954): a symbol of Catalan society based on 'bodily harmony and moral discretion'.

The Galician literary revival (*Rexurdimento*) dates from the 1863 publication of *Galician Songs* (*Cantares gallegos*) by Rosalía de Castro (1837–85): the first book of poetry published in Galician since the demise of Galician-Portuguese as the language of lyric poetry throughout much of the peninsula. The illegitimate daughter of a priest, Castro was brought up in the Galician countryside where Galician was spoken; she was an invaluable asset to her husband, Manuel Murguía, the 'father' of Galician nationalism, as a rare example of an intellectual who, unlike himself, spoke what had become the language of the peasantry. It has been noted that her use of Galician bears traces of Castilian; her

6. Rosalía de Castro with her husband Manuel Murguía and their children

Galician-language poetry is the expression, not of a 'pure' Galician identity, but of the living between languages that characterizes Galicia as a bilingual community. Her fiction (see Chapter 3) was written in Castilian. Criticized in 1881 for her unorthodox representation of Galician popular sexual customs, she vowed never to write in Galician again. Her last book of poetry, *En la orillas del Sar* (1884), although written in Castilian, retains the concern in all her poetic work with Galician nature and the peasantry, drawing on popular Galician song. She is a classic example of the Herderian ideal of literature as the expression of the *Volk*, the difference being that, in her case, she actually knew them. She also complicates the geographical boundaries of 'Galicianness' by focusing on Galicia's history of emigration; some of her poetry was published with financial assistance from the large Galician community in Havana. Her example encouraged the publication of other poetic works in Galician, all constructing a mournful vision of the Galician landscape: *Airs of My Land* (*Aires da miña terra*, 1880) by Manuel Curros Enríquez (1851–1908); *Galician Longings* (*Saudades gallegas*, 1880) by Valentín Lamas de Carvajal (1849–1906); and *Laments of the Pines* (*Queixumes dos pinos*, 1886) by Eduardo Pondal (1835–1917), which provided the lyrics of the Galician national anthem. This poetic production confirmed the traditional view of Galician as a language suited exclusively to lyric poetry, but it brought lyric poetry out of the intimate realm into the political arena.

Late 19th-century Basque nationalism could not call on a written literary tradition in the vernacular; *euskara*, fragmented dialectally, was spoken only by sectors of the peasantry. Consequently, the Basque literary revival privileged oral culture, particularly the vibrant tradition of poetic improvization (*bertsolaritza*), with folksongs and folktales being collected in anthologies. The founder of Basque nationalism in the 1880s to 1890s, Sabino Arana, was not a native speaker of Basque but learned and promoted the language, whose antiquity and unknown origins had made it a topic of discussion by European philologists, including Wilhelm von Humboldt (brother of the naturalist Alexander famed for his travels in South America), in the early 19th century.

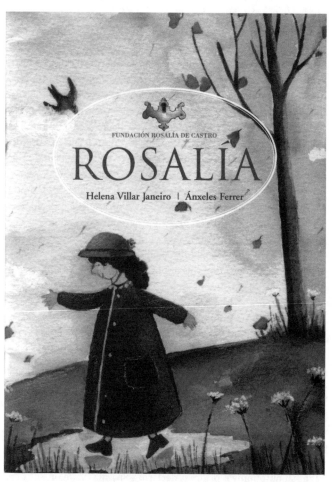

FUNDACIÓN ROSALÍA DE CASTRO

ROSALÍA

Helena Villar Janeiro | Ánxeles Ferrer

Front cover of a children's book of Rosalía de Castro's poetry (2008)

Non-state nationalisms played a significant political role in early
20th-century Spain, provoking a right-wing Spanish nationalist
backlash, first with the 1923–30 dictatorship of General Miguel
Primo de Rivera (himself a Catalan), which suppressed the Catalan

Multilingualism and porous borders

General Assembly (Mancomunitat) created by the Regionalist League in 1914; and then with the 1936 Nationalist military uprising led by General Francisco Franco which initiated the three-year Spanish Civil War. A key grievance of the right-wing coalition that supported the Nationalist uprising was the 1931–9 Spanish Republic's granting of autonomy to Catalonia in 1932, followed by Basque autonomy in 1936 (after the war's start); plans for Galician autonomy were stalled by Galicia's early fall to the military rebels. On the Republic's defeat by Franco's troops in April 1939, Catalan and Basque autonomy were abolished. Brutal political and cultural repression attempted to eradicate all opposition to the authoritarian state, which modelled itself on the Catholic Monarchs, inaccurately credited in Francoist ideology with implementing a premeditated programme of national unification through the suppression of local autonomy and imposition of Catholicism and Castilian culture. (As noted above, religious homegenization was not imposed till 1528, administrative unification till 1716, and linguistic unification till 1768.) In 1941, all languages other than Castilian (including foreign languages) were banned from public use. The ban on publication and performance in Catalan was lifted in 1946, though heavy censorship continued to limit Catalan public expression severely. By the 1960s, Catalan publishing houses were expanding, and literary production in Galician and *euskara* was emerging, though Castilian remained the sole official language of education for the Franco dictatorship's duration.

Not surprisingly, the 1978 Constitution, which consolidated the return to democracy after General Franco's death in 1975, made regional autonomy a priority, declaring Spain a 'State of Autonomous Governments' (*Estado de las Autonomías*). In 1980, home rule was instituted in Catalonia and the Basque Country, and approved for Andalusia and Galicia, with Spain's remaining regions following. Since the 1978 Constitution, 'Spain' means a nation-state built on the recognition of political devolution, though there is still friction over Catalan demands for increased autonomy plus the continuing problem of the Basque separatist terrorist group ETA (Basque Homeland and Freedom [Euskadi ta Askatasuna]). Cultural autonomy has theoretically been achieved, with Catalan, Galician, and Basque instituted as official languages of the Spanish state alongside Castilian. But in practice, bilingualism operates only in Catalonia, Galicia, and the Basque Country. Education in Catalonia and Galicia is in Catalan and Galician respectively, with the teaching of Spanish obligatory. In the Basque Country, given the smaller number of Basque speakers, some schools provide education in Basque and others in Spanish; all teach both languages. Basque-, Catalan-, and Galician-language television channels were created in 1983, 1984, and 1985, respectively. However, competition by Spanish-language television channels (state and private) remains an issue, given unequal resources. Newspapers published in the vernacular also have to compete with the Castilian-language press. While this competition is often lamented as inhibiting the hegemony of the vernacular, it makes Catalonia, Galicia, and the Basque Country truly bilingual societies.

Although the revival of literature in the vernacular started under the Franco regime in all three of Spain's historic nationalities, only in Catalonia did this produce a significant output, thanks partly to Barcelona's role as the hub of the Spanish publishing industry under the dictatorship. The nationalist agenda underlying much literary production in Catalan, Galician, and Basque has meant that, contrary to the multilingualism of the Middle Ages, there is little cultural exchange between the country's four officially recognized languages, the focus in each autonomous community being on its own vernacular. While this is understandable after over two centuries of enforced Castilianization, the privileging of local culture – evidenced in school literary curricula and literary prizes – has its risks. This privileging of local culture, it must be stressed, is found in all the autonomous regions, not just Catalonia, Galicia, and the Basque Country. Conversely, Spain's prestigious National Fiction Prize (Premio Nacional de Narrativa) shows uneven recognition of non-Castilian literatures: it has been awarded to three writers in Galician (Alfredo Conde, 1986; Manuel Rivas, 1996; Suso de Toro, 2003), two in Basque (Bernardo Atxaga, 1989; Unai Elorriaga, 2002), and, extraordinarily, only once to a writer in Catalan (Carme Riera, 1995), though at least she is one of only two women to have won this prize since the return to democracy (the other being the Castilian-language writer Carmen Martín Gaite, in 1978).

An issue here is how to classify Catalan, Galician, and Basque authors who write in Castilian. They tend to be excluded from discussion of Catalan, Galician, and Basque literature. This produces complications in the case of writers who have published in both languages: for example, the poet Pere Gimferrer (1945–) who in the 1970s switched from Castilian to Catalan; or the novelist Terenci Moix (1942–2003) who in 1983 switched from Catalan to Castilian (with one 1992 novel in Catalan). Writers who started to publish under the early Franco dictatorship, when Castilian was the only option, inevitably write in that language: for example, the Galician novelist Gonzalo Torrente Ballester (1910–99), or Catalan writers such as the poet Jaime Gil de Biedma (1929–90), the highly popular fiction and political writer Manuel Vázquez Montalbán (1939–2003), or the novelists Juan Goytisolo (1931–) and Juan Marsé (1933–). Marsé has angered Catalan nationalists by championing Catalan authors' right to write in Castilian, which in his case is largely about remaining faithful to his working-class origins, having been brought up in a Barcelona neighbourhood of southern Spanish immigrants to which he returns repeatedly in his fiction. The choice to write in Catalan, Galician, or Basque inevitably limits writers' readership. The two most recent bestseller writers, Carlos Ruiz Zafón (1964–), author of *The Shadow of the Wind* (*La sombra del viento*, 2001), and Ildefonso Falcones (1958–), author of *Cathedral of the Sea* (*La catedral del mar*, 2006), are both Catalans but chose to write in Castilian.

This is a particularly difficult choice in the case of Basque, which has a smaller readership (there are around one million speakers of *euskara*, including the French Basque Country – which raises another issue of borders). Bernardo Atxaga (1951–) is one of the few writers in *euskara* to have achieved international status: his stories *Obabakoak* (meaning 'Inhabitants of Obaba', 1988) won not only Spain's National Fiction Prize but also the Critics' Prize (Premio de la Crítica), the Basque Euskadi Prize, and the French Prix Millepages, and have been translated into over twenty languages (including Castilian, by himself). His later novels *The Lone Man* (*Gizona bere bakardadean* – Spanish translation *El hombre solo*, 1993), *The Lone Woman* (*Zeru horiek* – Spanish translation *Esos cielos*, 1996), and *The Accordionist's Son* (*Soinujolearen semea* – Spanish translation *El hijo del acordeonista*, 2003), have all been enthusiastically received and translated into English. But outside the Basque Country, he remains known largely as the author of *Obabakoak*, which attracted attention as the first fictional work in Basque to break with the habit of depicting Basque rural traditions. Obaba is a kind of Macondo, generating intertwining stories in the magical realist vein popularized by García Márquez and refusing any obvious 'Basqueness'. *The Lone Man*, *The Lone Woman*, and *The Accordionist's Son* all deal with characters trying to disentangle themselves from a history of Basque terrorist involvement: all are superbly complex political novels that make Atxaga perhaps the most important writer to have emerged from Spain in the last 30 years. Non-Basque readers seem to prefer him as the writer of less threatening stories.

Exiles and expatriates

We have seen how writers frequently crossed borders in medieval Iberia. Since 1492, the various attempts to suppress cultural diversity have led to successive waves of exiles; a considerable amount of 'Spanish literature' has thus been written overseas. In some cases, exile writers' work has been recuperated as part of

Spain's cultural heritage; in other cases, it is ignored (particularly the part written abroad). The recuperation process can be problematic if it simply reinserts writers into the Spanish pantheon as if their exile had never happened. This chapter has stressed the multilingualism and multiculturalism of much Spanish writing in order to question 'national' definitions of literature. Exile writers complicate such definitions further.

How, for example, do we deal with the peripatetic life of León Hebreo (c. 1465–c. 1523) – or should we use his Jewish name Judah Leon Abravanel, his Latin name Leo Hebraeus, his Portuguese name Leão Hebreu, or his Italian name Leone Ebreo? Born in Lisbon to Castilian Jewish parents who were forced to flee back to Castile in 1481, he became personal physician to the Catholic Monarchs in 1484. When in 1492 all Jews who refused to convert were expelled from Spain, he chose exile, settling in Italy. There, in 1501–2, having mixed with Italian humanist circles, he wrote the Neoplatonic love treatise that would be hugely influential in acclimatizing Renaissance humanism in Spain: *Love Dialogues* (*Dialoghi d'amore*), published in Italian, though he may have written it in his first language, Castilian. Clearly, no one nation can claim him. But if none claims him, what happens then? Another case is the humanist Juan Luis Vives (1493–1540), who opted for exile because of his *converso* origins, his father being burnt at the stake in 1524. He lived most of his life in Bruges, in the 1520s tutoring the young Mary Tudor in England, and writing in Latin.

In the modern period, a classic case is the early 19th-century Spanish liberal exile José María Blanco White (1775–1841), born in Seville to an Irish father and Spanish mother. On Napoleon's 1808 invasion of Spain, he patriotically chose to defend the Spanish cause, despite his conviction that Napoleonic rule would bring the liberal reforms he supported. When French troops took Seville in 1810, he fled to London, where many Spanish liberal exiles gathered. Unlike the others, he integrated into English literary society, founding a Spanish-language magazine *The Spaniard*

(*El Español*) but also writing for English journals, including J. S. Mill's *London and Westminster Review*. His major works, written in English, are his *Letters from Spain* (1822, composed for the *Quarterly Review*) and his autobiography *The Life of Joseph Blanco White Written by Himself* (posthumous, 1845). Ordained a Catholic priest in Spain but increasingly alienated by the Catholic Church's political and moral conservatism, in England he converted to Anglicanism (1812) and later Unitarianism (1835). This intellectual restlessness, mirroring his geographical dislocation, is reflected in all his writing. Until recently, no national literature has wanted to claim him. His work in English is still not entirely available in Spanish, though 1972 saw the translation of *Letters from Spain* and of selections from his autobiography and articles. The latter included a long preface by Juan Goytisolo, whose 1975 novel *Juan the Landless* (*Juan sin tierra*) takes as its title one of Blanco White's pen-names. The Spanish liberal exiles who returned to Spain have been reclaimed by Spanish literary histories. But we should remember that the flagship drama of Spanish Romanticism, *Don Álvaro or the Force of Destiny* (*Don Álvaro o la fuerza del destino*) – best known in Verdi's operatic version – by Ángel Saavedra, Duque de Rivas (1791–1865), was written in exile in French, three years before its 1835 Madrid performance. So too was *Aben-Humeya*, by his fellow Romantic dramatist, Francisco Martínez de la Rosa (1789–1862), much more successful at its 1830 first performance in Paris than at its 1836 Spanish premiere.

By far the largest cohort of exiles were the Spanish Republican supporters forced to leave by Nationalist victory in the Spanish Civil War: an estimated half million Spaniards fled, the majority ending in Spanish America (especially Mexico) but dispersed across Europe and the Americas. The vast majority of intellectuals had supported the Republic; the damage done to Spanish intellectual life by this exodus was immense. I do not have space here to do justice to the huge number of Republican exile writers, except to note that, of their works written in exile, those that tend to be read (if any) are those that deal with Spain. The alacrity with which those exile writers who returned to Spain (mostly after Franco's death in 1975) were reclaimed – for example, the poet Rafael Alberti (1902–99), or the novelists Rosa Chacel (1898–1994), Francisco Ayala (1906–2009), and Mercè Rodoreda (1908–83), the last now a major figure in the Catalan literary canon – suggests a desire to wipe out the memory of their years abroad, as if returning them to their pre-war origins. Little work has been done on Republican exiles' cultural relations with their host countries. An interesting case is Jorge Semprún (1923–) who, having left Spain as a boy, has written most of his literary output in French. *The Long Voyage* (*Le Grand voyage*, 1963), which recounts his internment in Buchenwald as a French Resistance fighter, is a classic of French literature. Yet Semprún's links with Spain remained strong, as organizer of the Spanish Communist Party's clandestine activities in Spain 1953–62 and Spanish Minister of Culture 1988–91. Semprún's novelized memoir *Autobiography of Federico Sánchez* (*Autobiografía de Federico Sánchez*, 1977) and historical novel *Twenty Years and a Day* (*Veinte años y un día*, 2003) are written in Spanish. Do these texts belong to Spanish literature while his works in French do not? Other cases are Fernando Arrabal (1932–), self-exiled in France since 1955, whose plays and novels have been performed or published in French, though he wrote most of his work in Castilian; or the novelist Juana Salabert (1962–), a second-generation exile born and brought up in France, who writes in Spanish. Spain was also host country to a number of exile writers from Latin America's Southern Cone during the military dictatorships of the 1970s to 1980s; a few, such as the Uruguayan writer Cristina Peri Rossi (1941–), have stayed in Spain. We should also remember that the novels of the Latin American 'boom' (1960s to 1970s) were largely published in Barcelona.

An increasing number of Spanish writers have become expatriates or 'lifestyle migrants'. In the late 1960s and early 1970s, many budding Spanish writers spent several years abroad, often in 'swinging London'. The first fictional work *Tales of Insubstantiality* (*Relatos sobre la falta de sustancia*, 1977) of Álvaro Pombo (1939–) depicts suburban London where he lived from 1966 to 1977. The bestselling writer Carlos Ruiz Zafón, mentioned above, has lived in Los Angeles since 1993. Ray Loriga (1967–, Anglicized pen-name), whose *The Man Who Invented Manhattan* (*El hombre que inventó Manhattan*, 2004) is set in New York, has lived there since 2000. Antonio Muñoz Molina (1956–) has since 2004 combined Madrid with Manhattan, depicted in his *Manhattan Windows* (*Las ventanas de Manhattan*, 2004). Eduardo Lago (1954–), whose *Call Me Brooklyn* (*Llámame Brooklyn*) won the 2006 Nadal Prize in Spain, has lived in New York for over twenty years. A character in his novel is Felipe Alfau (1902–99), who emigrated to New York during World War I, producing two novels in English, of which *Locos: A Comedy of Gestures* (1928) won critical success in the United States when reissued in 1987 with an 'Afterword' by Mary McCarthy.

I end this chapter with Juan Goytisolo who, having left Spain for Paris voluntarily but for political reasons in 1956, stands somewhere between the position of exile and expatriate. He calls himself an 'exile': a term that confers intellectual kudos. Despite over 50 years of residence abroad, he has retained his reputation as Spain's major living author.

Goytisolo fulfils two key requirements for being considered a Spanish writer: his entire output is written in Castilian, and much of it is obsessed with Spain, even when it is set elsewhere. His writing is an attempt to free himself from his bourgeois, pro-Franco, Catholic upbringing. This is most evident in his trilogy *Marks of Identity* (*Señas de identidad*, 1966), *Count Julian* (*Reivindicación del conde don Julián*, 1970), and *Juan the Landless* (1975) – now marketed as a boxed set entitled *Trilogy of Evil* (*Trilogía del mal*) – which remain his best-known novels for their relentless destruction of the Franco regime's ideology of 'Spanishness'. Nonetheless, he is probably read more abroad than

8. Juan Goytisolo in his study in Marrakesh, 2006

in Spain – his first major Spanish award, the National Literature Prize (Premio Nacional de las Letras), was given only in 2008. His greater popularity abroad – leaving aside Spanish touchiness about his hatred of Spain – is partly because he is the only Spanish writer who has remained faithful to the experimentalism of the Latin American 'boom' writers. This gives his writing a cosmopolitanism which he has also cultivated at the level of content, with novels dealing with AIDS (*The Virtues of the Solitary Bird* [*Las virtudes del pájaro solitario*, 1988]), or the Gulf War (*Quarantine* [*La cuarentena*, 1991]), and war in Bosnia (*State of Siege* [*El sitio de los sitios*, 1995]). His novels routinely move between different cultural spaces, mostly non-Spanish though Spain is frequently imagined from them, employing the nomadism theorized as a subversive practice by Deleuze and Guattari. For example, *Landscapes after the Battle* (*Paisajes después de la batalla*, 1985) moves between Paris, Tangiers, Marrakesh, Cairo, and Istanbul. In *The Virtues of the Solitary Bird* and *Quarantine*, he incorporates Sufi mysticism.

A major plank of Goytisolo's rejection of his Spanish Catholic upbringing has been his espousal of Arab culture. After coming out as homosexual in 1965, he divided his life between Marrakesh and his lifelong partner, the writer Monique Lange, in Paris – on her death in 1996 making Marrakesh his permanent home. His work explicitly presents Arab culture as an antidote to his repressive Spanish upbringing, including its compulsory heterosexuality. While this could be seen as an example of the orientalism critiqued by Edward Said (the West's tendency to see the Arab world as a projection of its repressed desires and fears), his abundant political journalism – whether on the Middle East, Bosnia, or Moroccan immigration in Spain – is an explicit attack on Western anti-Islamic prejudice. His critique of orthodox Marxism, at a time when it represented the ideology of the anti-Franco opposition, caused friction in Spain. He broke his support for the clandestine Spanish Communist Party when it expelled Jorge Semprún in 1964, and his links with Communist Cuba when news emerged in the late 1960s of its homosexual labour camps (he purged *Marks of Identity* of its first edition's chapter set in Cuba). Satires of Marxist orthodoxy remain frequent in his work which, like the Blanco White he admires, rejects orthodoxies of all kinds. What probably makes his work least palatable in today's Spain, which has enthusiastically embraced neoliberal consumerism, is its uncompromising critique of Marxism's enemy, Western capitalism. Goytisolo's most recent novel is titled *The Exile from Here and There* (*El exiliado de aquí y allá*, 2008). *Juan the Landless* ends in Arabic, and he has described himself as a 'Mudejar'. He has frequently paid tribute to past Spanish literature that acknowledges cultural plurality; accordingly, he has declared himself to be of 'Cervantine' rather than Spanish nationality.

Chapter 2
Spanish literature and modernity

There is no single definition of modernity. The most frequent meaning is that of capitalist modernization, involving industrialization and urbanization. This is usually complemented by the cultural notion of secularization, what Max Weber called 'disenchantment of the world'. Such definitions locate modernity's beginnings in 18th-century empiricism, which generated modern scientific enquiry. But there are other definitions, largely cultural. The most pervasive equates modernity with the break with a past perceived as fixed, inaugurating a perception of change and insecurity but also opportunity. This has been located at two different moments. First, the Enlightenment with its notion, essential to liberal political philosophy, of the autonomous individual or self-made man (not woman), which broke with political absolutism. Second, the Renaissance when humanist scholarship, drawing on Greek philosophy which reached the West partly via Muslim Iberia, challenged the absolute truths that supposedly characterized medieval culture by placing man at the centre of the universe, allowing the possibility of self-fashioning. Such beliefs were enhanced by the colonization of the New World, first undertaken by Spain. In the second case, the break is with a Middle Ages perceived as monolithic and stable; Chapter 1 should have shown that the Middle Ages were not like that at all. A further definition of modernity, political in origin but cultural in its effects, equates it with the emergence of the central state and its disciplinary mechanisms, which – as Foucault has shown – created subjects through its techniques of subjection. Both of these last two definitions make empire central to modernity.

If we define modernity as capitalist modernization, then Spain did not get there till the late 19th century (in Catalonia and the Basque Country only), and did not fully make it till the economic take-off of the 1960s, still under the Franco dictatorship, followed by accelerated capitalist development since 1975. As for secularization, the Catholic Church has been a major force in Spanish history, but that does not mean that there was no space for debate: this chapter explores some of the dissenting voices. If we locate modernity's start in the Enlightenment, as is usual, we find a gap between the discourses circulating in Spain and the reality on the ground, but that gap has been hugely productive culturally at certain moments. If, however, we take modernity's start back to the Renaissance – the period historians call 'early modern' – then Spain's position changes dramatically for it was the major early modern imperial power. Moreover, the cultural homogenization instituted in the name of religious orthodoxy by the Spanish state after 1492 was, as the historian Eric Hobsbawm has noted, a precocious anticipation of the nation-formation process that would take place across Europe (Spain included) in the mid-to-late 19th century. Although Spain did not undergo political and linguistic unification till the 18th century, the rule of the Catholic Monarchs and particularly that of their Habsburg successors were marked by the increasing subjection of citizens to state control.

There are historical reasons why Spain 'fell off' the map of European modernity after having been at its centre. In the late 16th century, Spain's political enemy England circulated massive propaganda in the Low Countries, where Spain was fighting a war against Protestantism, accusing Spain of atrocities in the New World, thereby giving rise to the 'Black Legend'. The atrocities were real but the data was taken from the plea to the Spanish

Crown to end exploitation of the American Indians by the Spanish Dominican friar, Bartolomé de las Casas. This plea resulted in Crown legislation protecting the Indians (mostly ignored by Spanish settlers, however). The 1648 Treaty of Westphalia marked Spain's replacement as the major European power by France and England, while Spain's loss of what would become the Dutch Republic in 1581 allowed Amsterdam to replace Seville as the centre of Atlantic trade. From this point, the Dutch, English, and French intensify their own imperial efforts, which become constitutive of their claim to modernity while Spain's early modern empire is written out of the modern imperial narrative as 'barbaric'. As has been noted, this led to Spain's conversion from historical subject into historical object, visited avidly by 19th-century northern European cultural tourists who believed they were travelling back to the Middle Ages.

In this chapter, I will argue that the undoubtedly repressive nation-formation process that took place under the Catholic Monarchs and Habsburgs produced some extraordinarily modern literary results. I will also look at those historical moments when literary creativity was triggered by the disjunction between modern ideas and material backwardness, as well as at the anachronisms produced by censorship during the Franco dictatorship, and today's paradoxical affirmation of modern democratic values through the cultural return to the past. I will start with a story of beginnings: modernity's key trope.

Constructing origins

We have seen how the 1948 discovery of the *kharjas* led to claims that the earliest recorded Romance literature was not after all in Occitan but in Ibero-Romance. The northern European construction of Spain as 'unmodern' has produced an anxiety about 'belatedness' which dogs the whole history of Spanish literary criticism. In repeatedly accusing Spanish authors of imitating foreign models, Spanish critics have internalized the hegemonic European narrative which assumes that this is the case. The other side of this is a chronic hypersensitivity to any suggestion that Spanish literature might not be 'original'. Also in 1948, the eminent Spanish literary scholar Ramón Menéndez Pidal argued defensively that, if Spanish literature (meaning Castilian literature) was a series of '*frutos tardíos*' (late-ripening fruits), that gave them 'more flavour'. In the late 20th century, Menéndez Pidal was accused of manipulating evidence to give the earliest possible date for the *Poem of the Cid* (*Poema de mio Cid*) which, thanks to his efforts, became Spain's foundational national epic. This 'creative dating' allowed him to counter suggestions of influence by the much larger corpus of French epic poetry. Around 297 French epics have been conserved, the earliest being *Song of Roland* (*Chanson de Roland*, *c.* 1100–70); Castilian has three, the other two being mid-13th and mid-14th century. Menéndez Pidal argued that the date 1245 (modern calendar 1207) given in the *Poem of the Cid*'s sole surviving 14th-century manuscript was an error for 1345, which made the name next to the date – Abbot Peter (Per Abbat) – that of the 14th-century copyist. Menéndez Pidal then argued that the surviving manuscript was a copy of an 1140 original, placing the *Poem of the Cid*'s composition only slightly later than the *Song of Roland*'s earliest dating. He then posited that this 1140 manuscript was based on a *c.* 1105 oral version composed shortly after the Cid's death in 1099. Menéndez Pidal went on to 'demonstrate' the existence of a substantial lost corpus of Castilian epic through his ingenious reading of Castilian chronicles, arguing that their prosody revealed certain passages to be based on lost epic verse, presumed to be part of an oral tradition stretching back to the time of the events depicted. Where I have used the term 'Castilian', Menéndez Pidal routinely uses the term 'Spanish'.

In the 1980s, the British Hispanist Colin Smith attacked Menéndez Pidal's *Cid* scholarship. Smith proposed Abbot Peter, the name given in the extant manuscript, as the poem's author, making it a learned work composed in 1207, which in his view showed evidence of French influence and legal training. But Smith also fell into the trap of wanting to argue for a 'first', since his suggestion that the poem was a learned work, rather than the transcription of an oral original, allowed him to declare Abbot Peter the first 'Spanish' author whose name is known – predating the usual claimant Gonzalo de Berceo (1196?–1264?), whose hagiographic and Marian verse was written in the 1230s to 1260s. Smith's investment in the modern concept of original authorship was as great as Menéndez Pidal's in the notion of oral composition. The latter's nationalistic arguments went together with his ardent championship of popular literature, on Herderian but also democratic grounds – he supported the Spanish Republic but returned to Franco's Spain from exile in 1940.

Menéndez Pidal's 'exhumation' and 'reconstruction' of the lost 'corpus' of Castilian oral epic, undertaken in his aptly titled *Relics of Spanish Epic Poetry* (*Reliquias de la poesía épica española*, 1951), have been hailed as a brilliantly imaginative act of mourning for a lost past. Scholars are still divided about the existence or not of a 'Spanish' oral epic tradition; most see the *Poem of the Cid* as a learned composition probably of the late 12th century. The time-lag with relation to France is thus generally accepted. Now that postcolonial studies, with their stress on inter-ethnic relations, allow Iberia's multicultural Middle Ages to be valued positively, Spanish scholars no longer have to worry about whether the lateness and paucity of Castilian epic production makes 'Spanish literature' 'inferior'.

A precocious modernity

Critics inspired by Foucault and by postmodern and postcolonial theory have produced some outstanding recent work on Spanish Golden Age literature, reconfiguring the field. Here, I discuss the debates on how literary texts dialogue with the early modern nation-formation process, through their often critical representation of it.

The instruments of centralized state power mobilized by the Catholic Monarchs and their Habsburg successors were the Holy Brotherhood (Santa Hermandad) created in 1476, and the Inquisition, established in 1478 under Spanish Crown (rather than Papal) control, although its mission was the eradication of heresy. The Holy Brotherhood comprised a constabulary and judicial tribunal that – like the modern Civil Guard (Guardia Civil) created in 1844 to enforce another nation-formation process – was charged with patrolling Spain's highways and rural areas, subjecting to state jurisdiction territory previously under local control. Several Golden Age authors had brushes with the law, including Cervantes, Mateo Alemán (1547–1615?), Francisco de Quevedo (1580–1645), and Fray Luis de León (1527–91). The last, of Jewish descent, was imprisoned by the Inquisition. The state's obsession with blood purity (*limpieza de sangre*) placed anyone of Jewish or Muslim descent under suspicion, even if their ancestors had converted to Christianity generations before. The Toledo blood purity statute and the first Spanish Index of Prohibited Books were issued in 1547, Cervantes' birth date (other blood purity statutes had operated since the century's start). A significant number of writers were of Jewish descent (*conversos*), many Jews being urban professionals, whereas the Moriscos largely worked in agriculture. *Converso* writers included (in addition to Fray Luis): Fernando de Rojas (c. 1465–1541), author of *Celestina*; the picaresque novelist Mateo Alemán; possibly Cervantes; and St John of the Cross and St Teresa of Avila (see Chapter 3). In the 1480s, Rojas's father was convicted by the Inquisition of Judaizing practices, and six other relatives were forced to recant publicly in *autos-de-fé*. The strikingly modern nihilism of *Celestina* (1499) may relate to this.

Spanish citizens were, then, constantly required to produce a family history to prove that their lineage was untainted. The result was a new sense of identity shaped by the interpellations of the state. Foucault has shown the centrality of confession – the basis of inquisitorial procedure – to the modern sense of self. The low-life delinquent protagonists of the picaresque novel – named after its *pícaro* (rogue) protagonists – address their first-person life-story to an unknown authority figure or, in the case of *Guzmán de Alfarache*, to the reader cast as judge. It has been suggested that the modern novel born in Spain with the picaresque genre, and later *Don Quixote*, is a realist genre because of its relationship to the law, which probed everyday behaviour to determine religious orthodoxy.

The protagonists of the picaresque novel – *Lazarillo de Tormes* (1554, anon.), *Guzmán de Alfarache* (Part I: 1599, Part II: 1604) by Mateo Alemán, *The Swindler* (*El buscón*, 1626), by Quevedo – confess in their first-person narratives to racially tainted pedigrees. Lazarillo's mother set up with a black Muslim, as a result of which the young Lazarillo is interrogated and his mother flogged publicly. Guzmán, writing his life-story while serving a life sentence in the galleys for theft, has a probably *converso* father who, while held captive in Algiers, reneged and married a Muslim, absconded with her wealth and reconverted to Christianity so as to return to Spain, where he fathered Guzmán in an adulterous relationship (he is also rumoured to be homosexual, another crime punishable by the Inquisition). Pablos, the protagonist of *The Swindler*, has a *converso* mother reputed to be a witch and whore, sentenced by the Inquisition to be flogged to death. (A recently discovered anti-Jewish pamphlet by Quevedo was published in 1996.)

Lazarillo, composed in the mid-16th century, invites laughter as its protagonist tricks his various masters, exposing them as greater rascals than himself. Thanks to his native wit, he achieves financial security married to an archpriest's housekeeper in a *ménage à trois*. *Guzmán*, written at the end of the century, has a darker tone, with its anti-hero, due to his own defects, sinking ever lower. *The Swindler*, written in the early 17th century though published (unauthorized) only in 1626, is vicious in its criticism of all and sundry, though Pablos goes unpunished and at the end is preparing to try his luck in the Americas. This darkening of tone can be explained by the proliferation of Poor Laws (mentioned in *Lazarillo*) from the 1520s to the 1590s, accompanied by intensifying debates over how to deal with vagrants. The Church's traditional line in these debates was that poverty was a moral issue, the remedy being Christian charity. The poor should thus be allowed to beg freely. But a number of reformers argued for state intervention to round up vagrants, confining them and making them productive (including as Crown galley-slaves, Guzmán's fate). A number of workhouses were created during this period. Alemán, author of *Guzmán de Alfarache*, was a friend of the major reformer, the physician Cristóbal Pérez de Herrero, who recommended creating state-funded institutions to house the indigent: this was a bid for secular (and medical) control of the poor, removing them from Church protection. His proposals resonate uncannily with the debates on social control in late 19th-century Spain, the period of the realist novel (see below). They anticipate by a century the French discourses of social control studied by Foucault as the starting-point of modern disciplinary regimes.

As in late 19th-century Spain, a prime concern was how to distinguish between the deserving and undeserving poor. By the late 16th century, the poor had come to be seen as delinquents. In a letter to Pérez de Herrero, Alemán (a government inspector) declared that his aim in writing his novel was to help distinguish between the genuine and fraudulent poor, so the former could receive protection. *Guzmán de Alfarache* is the most moralizing Spanish picaresque novel but was the bestseller of its day (beaten only by *Don Quixote* six years later); indeed, all these picaresque novels were widely read in Spain and abroad. Their first-person accounts produce a double-voiced narrative: that of the plaintiff before the law, who must not tell an obvious lie but needs to present his case in a favourable light. Their highlighting of their narrative unreliability gives these texts a self-reflexive quality – a characteristic seen as the hallmark of the modern (and postmodern) novel. Ian Watt situated the rise of the novel in 18th-century England, but Defoe's *Moll Flanders* (1722) and Fielding's *Tom Jones* (1749) have 16th-century Spanish ancestors.

This self-reflexivity can be related to the ongoing expansion of the state bureaucratic machine which regulated Spain's vast American and European possessions. To cope with the proliferation of paper, in 1588 Philip II created the second state archive in Europe at Simancas (the first was the Archives of the Crown of Aragon, founded by James II of Aragon in 1318). Cervantes, like Alemán, was a state-employed record-keeper, from the late 1580s to 1600 travelling Andalusia to levy food supplies for the 1588 Invincible Armada and then as tax inspector. He was imprisoned twice for accounting irregularities – incidents that in themselves illustrate the gap between the written and the real. In Chapter 9 of *Don Quixote* Part I, the narrator tells us that what follows is the translation he commissioned from a Morisco of a manuscript in Arabic by a Moorish historian Cide Hamete Benengeli, with marginal comments in Arabic by an unknown reader, which he chanced upon about to be sold as scrap paper in Toledo's former Arab market (there is clearly too much paper around). This raises doubts about the rest of Part I's trustworthiness: not only is it a translation but the 1567 decree prohibiting use of Arabic declared all documents in that language legally null and void. Such self-reflexive touches open up a gap between representation and reality. Foucault's brilliant reading of *Don Quixote* in *The Order of Things* saw it as marking the passage from a Renaissance worldview based on similitude to a Baroque view based on representation. Don Quixote, who takes literally the Neoplatonic view of the world as book by trying to live out the novels of chivalry, is shown to be mad, for a gap has opened up between text and world which only he fails to recognize. The proliferation in the novel of stories within stories, with characters telling and listening to and commenting on stories (and in Part II commenting on Part I), shows that there is no one 'truth' but only multiple points of view, all of which are versions. This relativism is profoundly secular.

The sense of a gap between words and things is reinforced by late 16th- and 17th-century debates on Spain's growing inflation (the Crown suspended payments ten times between 1557 and 1662). Again uncannily anticipating the late 19th century, this period produced some extraordinarily modern economic critiques, attempting to explain why, when there was more money around (with the influx of American silver and the Crown's minting of additional coinage), it was worth less. The realization of the arbitrary, shifting relationship between the nominal value of money and its actual value on the market opens up another gap between representation and reality. This debate on the instability of monetary value, running from 1562 to 1640 and peaking in the 1590s, coincides with the high point of Golden Age literature. Foucault saw *Don Quixote* as anticipating a new worldview that would become general across Europe in the mid-17th century, but Cervantes' novel is the salient example of a tendency present in the whole of Spanish Golden Age literature, becoming particularly prominent at the 17th century's start.

A key aim of the new centralized state apparatus was to end the nobility's exemption from responsibility before the law. In the famous Golden Age dramas *Fuenteovejuna* (1612–14) and *Peribáñez* (1605?) by Lope de Vega (1562–1635), and Calderón's *The Mayor of Zalamea* (*El alcalde de Zalamea*, 1636), the Crown approves the execution of a nobleman by the villagers he has abused. Tirso de Molina's *The Trickster of Seville* ends with the King making amends to all the women Don Juan has dishonoured, demonstrating that, as a nobleman, Don Juan is not above the law. This curbing of the nobility's privileges meant the replacement of chivalric values – the honour code – by state authority. This is the crucial context to the critique of Don Quixote's knightly ethos: after freeing the galley slaves from the Holy Brotherhood, on the assumption that he is above the law, he becomes an outlaw on the run, as Sancho notes. His various other offences range from causing grievous bodily harm to damaging private property.

He is arrested at the end of Part I but deemed unfit to stand trial because he is mad.

The state's assertion of its jurisdiction over the whole population meant taking the regulation of morality away from the Church. The state became increasingly concerned with the arbitration of private life, exemplified in literature by love relations. The interpolated stories in *Don Quixote*, all love stories of some kind, turn the characters listening to them into a court of law arbitrating the moral dilemmas narrated. Perhaps the two most famous interpolated stories in *Don Quixote* are the captive's tale – in which a Spanish captain returns from captivity in Algiers with his Muslim bride-to-be and would-be Christian convert, Zoraida – and the story of the Morisco Ricote and his daughter Ana Félix. The latter ends with Ana Félix and her 'Old Christian' nobleman lover (who had devotedly followed her to North Africa) awaiting a Crown decision on whether they may marry, since she and her father have returned to Spain illegally after the Moriscos' expulsion in 1609–14. This expulsion took place between the publication of *Don Quixote*'s first and second parts (1605 and 1615). If the captive's tale in Part I is an orientalist fantasy which presents Zoraida's acceptance in Spain as unproblematic, Ricote's story, in Part II, treats highly topical, controversial material. Cervantes' captivity in Algiers (1575–80) after capture by Turkish pirates, and his loss of one hand's use in the 1571 Battle of Lepanto against the Turks, might have been expected to result in Islamophobia. But his experience of Algiers' polyglot society, populated by renegades from all over Europe, seems to have produced a sensitivity to cultural diversity and to the notion of culture as translation that anticipates the postmodern rejection of modernity's homogenizing impulse. Sympathy for Ricote and his daughter is explicit. We should, however, remember that the characters of Muslim descent that Cervantes depicts positively are all converts, or would-be converts, to Christianity.

Cervantes is one of many Golden Age writers fascinated with passing. Passing suggests that identity is performative rather than determined by biology (race or sex). Chapter 3 will discuss gender transvestism, but there is much ethnic cross-dressing as well. In order to sneak into Spain, Ricote is travelling disguised as a German pilgrim, and Ana Félix as a Turkish corsair captain which allows her to 'man' a ship. Her Christian lover is rescued from Algiers by a Spanish renegade who then converts back to Christianity: religions are donned and discarded in the same way that nationality depends on one's costume.

Throughout the 16th century, Moorish garments and goods were coveted luxury items. The late 16th and early 17th centuries saw a vogue for Morisco ballads (*romances moriscos*) and the Morisco novel (*novela morisca*), despite the 1568–71 Morisco Revolt. These texts are not just orientalist fantasies but the expression of a deeply hybridized culture: at least 300,000 Moriscos remained in Spain till their expulsion in 1609–14. Being both Spanish and Moorish, the Moriscos undo the state's exclusionary logic. The novella *El Abencerraje* (anon., most complete version 1565), depicts the chivalrous homosocial bond between a Christian and a Muslim knight. The two-volume *Civil Wars of Granada* (*Guerras Civiles de Granada*, 1595, 1619) by Ginés Pérez de Hita (1544?–1619?) straddles the expulsion date. Part I is presented as the author's translation of an Arabic text by a Spanish Muslim historian who left for North Africa in 1492 (and thus did not convert), whose grandson gave it to a Jewish Rabbi who translated it into Hebrew and gave the Arabic original to the Count of Bailén (known for opposing the Moriscos' expulsion), who then asked the Rabbi to translate it into Spanish (so he is a descendent of Spanish-speaking Jews exiled in 1492), but since the Count found the translation poor he gave it to Pérez de Hita. This outdoes Cervantes' later literary games in claiming that most of *Don Quixote* Part I is a translation of an Arabic original. But in one sense, this claim strengthens the text's veracity since its 'original author' witnessed the pre-1492 internecine fighting in Granada. In Part II, Pérez de

Hita claims this testimonial role for himself, having fought in the Spanish army that suppressed the Morisco Revolt. The fighting is explicitly presented as another Civil War since, as the narrator notes, the Spanish soldiers and the Moriscos are both Spaniards; both sides' viewpoints are given.

The intercultural communication represented in these texts escalates in Cervantes' Byzantine romance *Persiles and Sigismunda* (*Persiles y Sigismunda*, posthumous 1617), finished two days before his death. The narrator notes how the characters fail to understand one another since they speak different languages, including Castilian, Valencian, Portuguese, French, German, Italian, Irish, Norwegian, Polish, Lithuanian, Arabic, the renegade pidgin of Algiers, and the language of the 'Barbaric Isle'. Various polyglot characters serve as translators; the novel's text is allegedly translated from an unspecified language. The ongoing conversation between Don Quixote and Sancho has been seen as an example of the heteroglossia that, for Mikhail Bakhtin, was fundamental to the emergence of the novel, making it a democratic genre through its expression of plural viewpoints. The *Persiles* is literally heteroglossic as its protagonists, on their meandering journey from the Arctic to Rome, acquire a proliferation of travelling companions who tell their stories in different languages, 'translated' by Cervantes into Castilian.

It has been noted that the 'Barbaric Isle' in the *Persiles* sounds much like the New World as described by the Spanish conquistadors. The *Quixote* has been seen as a critique of imperial militaristic discourse, mocked in Don Quixote's chivalric obsession. The conquistadors compared the New World's marvels to the exotic lands traversed in *Amadís de Gaula*, from which the name 'California' is taken. Stephen Greenblatt has argued that wonder is the central trope of Europe's initial encounter with the New World. Wonder is also the central trope of the Spanish American Baroque – 'the marvellous real' (*lo real maravilloso*) as the 20th-century Cuban novelist Alejo Carpentier called it.

Influenced by surrealism, Carpentier meant by this the harnessing of incompatible opposites – in this case, the worldviews of colonizer and colonized. By contrast, the Spanish Baroque has been seen as a negative expression of Spain's growing 17th-century political and economic decadence: an excess masking a fear of the void (*horror vacui*). Recent postcolonial readings of the Spanish Baroque, however, interpret its emphasis on deceptive appearances (*engaño/desengaño*) as a category collapse which generates a modern sense of unstable, shifting identities.

The notion that identity is dependent on disguise is anticipated in 16th-century Spanish lyric poetry, which draws on the Petrarchan courtly love tradition, imported from Italy by Garcilaso de la Vega. The pastoral mode of Garcilaso's *Eclogues* gives rise to the pastoral novel genre, also hugely popular in 16th-century Spain: *La Diana* (c. 1559) by Jorge de Montemayor (1520?–61) and Cervantes' early *La Galatea* (1585). Although this pastoral world is based on a Neoplatonic vision of man in harmony with nature, in practice this harmony is broken by the unrequited love lamented by the male poet. It has been suggested that 16th-century lyric poetry – in Spain and England – provided a counter-discourse to the celebration of empire, allowing recognition of the unreciprocated (unrequited) nature of the colonizer's desire. Petrarchism also expressed a new form of moral and aesthetic self-making, countering the state's obsession with blood lineage as the benchmark of identity. This is achieved though its courtly characters masquerading as Arcadian shepherds and shepherdesses – another kind of passing. In the 16th century, the emphasis is on successful self-making. In the 17th century, self-fashioning comes to be viewed through a Baroque emphasis on false appearances, such that nothing can be trusted. This shift is visible in the difference between *Don Quixote* Parts I and II: Part I stresses Don Quixote's sincere attempts to pass as a knight of chivalry; Part II emphasizes the tricks played on him by other characters who deliberately fake chivalric scenarios.

In the Baroque, fraudulent assumed identities are not opposed to an 'authentic' self; all identities are 'faked' – that is, man-made. This chimes with Judith Butler's postmodern suggestion that all identity is performative. Many 17th-century writers were courtiers; they all needed courtly patronage. The increasingly lavish rituals of the 17th-century Spanish court, dominated by royal favourites whose rise and fall could be vertiginous, required courtiers to present an acceptable public façade; failure to do so meant loss of favour, if not imprisonment. Quevedo and especially Baltasar Gracián (1601–58) wrote numerous courtly conduct manuals: Quevedo's *Politics of God* (*Politica de Dios*, 1626/55), Gracián's *The Hero* (*El héroe*, 1637), *The Gentleman of Discretion* (*El discreto*, 1646), *The Art of Wordly Wisdom* (*Oráculo manual y arte de prudencia*, 1647), and *Skill and Art of Wit* (*Agudeza y arte de ingenio*, final version 1648). In Gracián's allegorical novel *The Sceptic* (*El criticón*, 1651–7), the protagonists – a man of the world and the 'natural man' he encounters when shipwrecked on an island – discuss their perceptions along their life-journey, elaborating a methodology of doubt which anticipates the modern 'disenchantment of the world'. Gracián's concept of the self as a 'caudal' (treasure) also anticipates Bourdieu's notion of cultural capital; the self is a resource that must be wisely exploited by being turned into a 'persona' – a mask, or social self. Gracián was a Jesuit: the 1548 *Spiritual Exercises* of the Jesuit's founder, St Ignatius of Loyola, constitute a handbook of Renaissance self-fashioning. Gracián, writing a century later, incurred sanction from his Jesuit superiors for proposing that doubt, rather than faith, was the key to knowledge. For Gracián, self-making is the construction of a fiction.

This Baroque notion of self-authoring as the construction of a false persona is perfectly illustrated by Tirso's *The Trickster of Seville*. As the play's title indicates, the focus is on the deceptions used by Don Juan to seduce women, rather than on the sexual acts themselves (for this reason, I do not consider Don Juan in the chapter on 'Gender and sexuality'). The theatricality of this self-making is brilliantly conveyed in Calderón's dramas, through their use of dialogue, structure (including plays within the play), and stage machinery to explore the deceptive nature of all perception. Perception becomes a matter of optics. Calderón's best-known play, *Life is a Dream* (*La vida es sueño*, 1635), does not oppose reality to illusion but shows that all experience is performative; that is, theatrical role-play. Although Calderón takes farthest the collapse of the reality/appearance distinction, it is fundamental to all Golden Age drama, in which actors play characters who regularly assume disguises. The title *Lo fingido verdadero* (*True Pretence*) of Lope de Vega's 1604 drama about St Genesius, the patron saint of actors who (in Lope's version) converted to Christianity in the course of acting a Christian convert's story, encapsulates this category collapse. A major Golden Age genre was the *auto sacramental* (morality play) performed for Corpus Christi, which became the Catholic calendar's major festival after the affirmation by the Council of Trent (1545–63) of the doctrine of Transubstantiation (the conversion of bread and wine into Christ's body during Mass). Transubstantiation may strike us as a very alien concept today, but it replicates the collapse of appearance and substance that makes Golden Age theatre seem so postmodern. Calderón's best-known *auto sacramental* is also titled *Life is a Dream*.

The poet most associated with the Baroque is Luis de Góngora (1561–1627). The monstrous – a word that appears frequently in Calderón's dramas – is central to Góngora's *Fable of Polyphemus and Galatea* (*Fábula de Polifemo y Galatea*, published posthumously, like all his work). His dislocated syntax mirrors the theme of shipwreck in his *Solitudes* (*Soledades*, incomplete). In both these poems, the self-fashioning of 16th-century pastoral is subjected to a linguistic distortion that produces disconcerting aesthetic effects. Their optical, theatrical nature requires the reader to reflect on the nature of perception. This is Baroque wonder not at God's creation (nature) but at the potential of the artistic imagination (artifice). The basis of this imagination is metaphor, which no longer expresses similitude (as in 16th-century Neoplatonism) but the violent yoking together of the dissimilar. We will see below how this resonated with the poetic concerns of Spain's 1920s avant-garde.

Writing the nation

Nation-formation, meaning capitalist modernization and state centralization, was the political goal of the Restoration period inaugurated in 1875 with the return of the Bourbon monarchy after the 'revolutionary years' which followed Spain's 1868 liberal revolution. This is the period of Spain's realist novel. But the realist novel builds on a long history, in the modern (as opposed to early modern) period, of reflections on the nation. The concern with Spain's economic backwardness, by comparison with the northern European powers that had 'robbed' it of major power status in the mid-17th century, had since then generated much political and economic debate, especially under the Enlightenment monarch Charles III (ruled 1759–88) whose reforms increased state centralization, remodelled urban space, and encouraged economic debating societies. Many literary texts of this time – for example, neoclassical dramas on national history – have aged badly thanks to their formal conservatism, despite being progressive politically. Most of those still read today elaborate a new form of bourgeois sensibility: for example, the Gothic *Lugubrious Nights* (*Noches lúgubres*, 1771) by José de Cadalso (1741–82).

National identity is, however, explored directly in Cadalso's *Moroccan Letters* (*Cartas marruecas*, 1789), which aims to counter Montesquieu's dismissal of Spain in his *Persian Letters* (*Lettres persanes*, 1721). French Enlightenment thinkers saw Spain as an indolent nation incapable of progress (the European stereotype of the Muslim world). Cadalso engages with this by presenting a fictitious exchange of letters between an educated Moroccan visitor to Spain, Gazel, and his friend back in Morocco, plus additional correspondence between them and Gazel's Spanish host. As in

Montesquieu's original, the pretence of foreign authorship allows expression of a *faux-naive* questioning of national customs. But the main effect of the pretence of Moroccan interlocutors is to establish that Spain is not like North Africa, for Gazel is constantly surprised by what he sees – for good and ill.

Romanticism entered Spain in 1814 with translation of the Schlegel brothers' literary writings (mentioned in the Introduction), which exalted Spanish Golden Age literature – dismissed by Spanish neoclassical thinkers – as a Herderian expression of Spanish popular sentiment, assumed to be monarchist and Catholic. For the Schlegel brothers, Spanish Golden Age literature represented the Counter-Reformation's attempt to combat Protestantism by preserving medieval values. This conservative nationalist reading of Spanish literature was attractive in Spain in 1814, the year when Napoleonic troops, which had occupied Spain in 1808, were defeated. Napoleon's invasion damaged Spanish liberalism irrevocably, as liberals – like Blanco White (see Chapter 1) – were forced to choose between joining the fight against Napoleon (which meant fighting for the absolutist monarch Ferdinand VII's return), or supporting Napoleon's brother Joseph Bonaparte, placed on the Spanish throne in 1808 (which meant supporting liberal reform but betraying one's country). The third option, chosen by many, was exile. It was not till 1833 that the politically progressive strand of Romanticism took Spain by storm, with the return of liberal exiles on Ferdinand VII's death. In the 1840s, after a decade of political turbulence, Spanish liberalism swung to the right.

The political tensions within Spanish Romanticism are seen in the Romantic historical novel's turn to the medieval past to imagine both conservative and progressive models of the nation. *The Lord of Bembibre* (*El señor de Bembibre*, 1844) by Enrique Gil y Carrasco (1816–45) replicates the Schlegels' exaltation of a Catholic Middle Ages. But the medieval heroes of *Don Enrique the Sad's*

Page (*El doncel de don Enrique el doliente*, 1834) by Mariano José de Larra (1809–37) and *Sancho Saldaña* (1834) by José de Espronceda are secular rebels in the mould of Byron's Cain. Larra had been brought up in France where his father, a liberal Bonapartist, was exiled; Espronceda, a liberal conspirator against Ferdinand VII, had returned from exile in London and Paris in 1833. For these progressive liberals, the Spanish Middle Ages represented a period when local and individual rights had not yet been curbed by the creation of a central state.

Spanish Romantics drew also on the country's medieval Muslim past, whether as foil to or illustration of the model of the nation proposed. In the play *The Lovers of Teruel* (*Los amantes de Teruel*, 1837), by Juan Eugenio Hartzenbusch (1806–80), Muslim Valencia, where the Christian hero Marsilla is initially held captive, represents the wealth whose acquisition allows him to rise socially, and a predatory female sexuality contrasting with the submissiveness of Marsilla's Christian betrothed, Isabel. The protagonists embody the ideals of the self-made man and the domestic 'angel of the hearth' central to bourgeois liberalism. By contrast, the previously mentioned Martínez de la Rosa's *Aben-Humeya*, which dramatizes the 1568–71 Morisco Revolt, makes its Morisco heroes defenders of freedom against an encroaching central state. The long narrative poem *The Moorish Foundling* (*El moro expósito*, 1834) by Ángel Saavedra (Duque de Rivas), which depicts the splendour of 10th-century Muslim Cordoba, does not so much elaborate a model of the nation as found it on an irreparable loss: that of a civilized Muslim Iberia. Halfway through the poem, the Muslim hero Mudarra (revealed as the bastard of a Castilian nobleman, captive in 10th-century Cordoba, and the Caliph's sister) leaves for Christian Burgos to avenge the deaths of his Castilian half-brothers, followed by his Muslim beloved, Kerima. Both, educated in Arabic philosophy and science, are shocked by Castile's lack of culture and militaristic ethos. The poem denies them (and Christian Castile) a happy end, for its narrative is built on a melancholic attachment to a lost past, which functions as a Benjaminian recovery of lost utopian potential.

The 1830s also saw the development of the *costumbrista* genre: press articles describing national customs. The *costumbrista* article was initiated by Mariano José de Larra in 1828, five years before Ferdinand VII's death, when he returned from France; his brilliant use of satire was necessary to beat the censors. His articles dissect what is backward in Spain as well as indicating the flaws in an incipient bourgeois modernity. Ramón Mesonero Romanos (1803–82), who would become Madrid's official chronicler (his library forms the nucleus of Madrid's Municipal Museum), paints a more jovial picture. During the 1830s to 1850s, Mesonero Romanos was responsible for the modernization of Madrid's urban space. His press articles, written 1832–42, track his strolls round the city as *flâneur*. He is documenting the 'typical' local customs that his urban reforms would eliminate.

The documentary impulse to 'map the city' is fundamental to the urban novels of Spain's major realist writer, Benito Pérez Galdós (1843–1920), particularly from *The Disinherited* (*La desheredada*, 1881) which follows its protagonist Isidora round Madrid, from city centre to working-class outskirts. The 1880s were a time of intense public discussion in Spain, drawing on the latest European political and social thinking. The gap between a desired modernity and its lack on the ground is what impels the debates; the Spanish realist novel is their literary extension. A key topic was the need for social reform, with vagrants and prostitutes singled out as a problem (as elsewhere in Europe). Isidora becomes a prostitute; her brother Mariano is a street-child who at the end awaits confinement in a new model reformatory. The novel's tours of Madrid's lunatic asylum, where their father dies, and the women's prison, where Isidora is interned, plead for reformed sanitary conditions. The character who tries to save Isidora is a doctor, reflecting the medical profession's leading role in the reform process, with which Galdós had close ties.

9. Benito Pérez Galdós's study at his summer home San Quintín, Santander

Most of these social reformers were linked to the Krausists: philosophers and educators influenced by Hegel's German contemporary Krause, who shared Hegel's concern with ethics but not his enthusiasm for the state. The Krausists became the champions in Restoration Spain of individual and local freedoms being eroded by a modernizing central state; they also attacked Church power. Their solution was private, secular reform initiatives. The Church, faced by this threat to its traditional management of the poor, encouraged religious philanthropy, leading to the foundation of a number of Magdalen houses. The competition between religious and freethinking reformers produced an invasion of the private lives of the working classes – ironically, given the Krausists' belief in individual autonomy. This invasion of privacy is reflected in Galdós's best-known novel, *Fortunata and Jacinta* (*Fortunata y Jacinta*, 1886–7), with the convent reformatory for prostitutes and the bossy philanthropist,

Guillermina, who both try to 'reform' Fortunata. Indeed, almost everyone in the novel tries to 'civilize' her – that is, incorporate her into the bourgeois nation for their own benefit. *La Regenta* (1884–5), by the leading Krausist political thinker and journalist Leopoldo Alas (1852–1901, pen-name 'Clarín') criticizes philanthropic efforts by both Church and freethinkers through the propaganda battle for control of a dying alcoholic pauper waged by the male protagonist, the priest Fermín, and the local atheist. Galdós's novels of the 1890s – *Ángel Guerra* (1890–1), *Nazarín* (1895), *Halma* (1895) – depict religious idealists' independent philanthropic attempts, free of both state and Church control. Their saintly refusal to distinguish between deserving and undeserving poor proves deluded but is contrasted favourably with bourgeois social rationalization.

Galdós's novels also criticize consumerism and its inverse, hoarding. In *Fortunata and Jacinta*, the bourgeois Santa Cruz family – whose son Juanito repeatedly seduces and abandons Fortunata – made their money in textile retailing, as did the family of Juanito's wife Jacinta; Juanito's mother is always out shopping. Fortunata and her petty-bourgeois husband Maxi live with his aunt Doña Lupe, a penny-pinching moneylender; the latter's moneylender friend Torquemada (named after the notorious Inquisitor) is the protagonist of four Galdós novels from 1889 to 1895. Money determines the plot of *That Bringas Woman* (*La de Bringas*, 1884), which charts its bourgeois heroine Rosalía's engulfment by debt, thanks to seduction by the latest fashions. Rosalía's miserly husband hoards banknotes. In critiquing consumption, Galdós is expressing contemporary anxieties about the depletion of natural resources, the 'natural' Fortunata – 'consumed' by a range of bourgeois characters – being their embodiment. In critiquing hoarding, he is exposing the absurdity of fetishing money which has an unstable, arbitrary relation to value.

The 1880s saw major debate in Spain about escalating national debt and inflation, and about the increasing reliance on paper

10. Benito Pérez Galdós

money, whose material value is worthless. Issue of paper money spiralled between 1871 and 1883. After the 1881 Barcelona Stock Exchange crash – chronicled in the Catalan realist novel *Gold Fever* (*La febre d'or*, 1890–3) by Narcís Oller – Spain abandoned the gold standard in 1883 when most other Western nations were adopting it. This meant that paper money could no longer be exchanged for gold; the value of money had become entirely free-floating. Late 20th-century economists have praised this decision as ahead of its time; in its day, it caused huge concern. Money is central to Galdós's novels not only because of their emphasis on material reality, but also because contemporary debates showed how, in the modern capitalist market system, the value of things is determined not by their material substance but by their monetary value on the market. Monetary value, as paper money shows, is pure representation. Many critics have commented on the highly self-reflexive nature of Galdós's realism, thanks to his love of Cervantine unreliable narrators. As in Cervantes' day, this self-reflexivity is linked to debates on the arbitrariness of monetary representation. Galdós's most self-reflexive novel, *La de Bringas*, was written the year after Spain abandoned the gold standard. His novels – not unlike 17th-century Baroque literature – are peopled with characters whose social worth is determined by their external appearance: in *Fortunata and Jacinta*, Galdós called fashion the key to contemporary history.

To bring in income, as one of Spain's first purely professional writers, Galdós wrote 46 *National Episodes* (*Episodios nacionales*, 1873–9, 1898–1912) tracking Spain's history from the Battle of Trafalgar (1805) to the Restoration's start. These historical novels literally 'write the nation', giving an increasingly critical account. Their huge success did much to convert readers into members of a national 'imagined community'. But Galdós's contemporary novels, with their vast canvas of characters crossing all social classes, offer a better example of the 'slice of life' that Benedict Anderson has shown to be the realist novel's key contribution to modern nation-formation: a replica of the nation whose inhabitants mostly do not meet but whose destinies are entwined in ways that escape their individual understanding.

The shock of the new

This section looks at the 1920s avant-garde. Early 20th-century Spanish fiction – excepting Unamuno's novels discussed in

Chapter 3 – remains largely realist. Some novels depict urban alienation, including that of the working classes, as in the trilogy *The Struggle for Life* (*La lucha por la vida*, 1904–5) of Pío Baroja (1872–1956). But most explore the lack of modernization (or the negative consequences of capitalist modernity grafted onto abject poverty) in the rural areas, stressing sexual repression, as in Baroja's *Way of Perfection* (*Camino de perfección*, 1902) and Azorín's *The Will to Live* (*La voluntad*, 1902), or the social novels of Vicente Blasco Ibáñez (1867–1928), Felipe Trigo (1864–1916), and Concha Espina (1869–1955). The 1920s see an explosion of experimental writing which takes the city as the cipher of modernity. It has been noted that the most brilliant avant-gardes occurred not in the most advanced nations but in those characterized by uneven development. What produced the 'shock of the new' central to avant-garde aesthetics was the coexistence of apparently incompatible temporalities. Most members of Spain's 1920s avant-garde came to Madrid from the rural periphery: the newly discovered modern city is not only the subject of much of their work but shapes its modes of perception. When forms and motifs of popular poetry are harnessed to avant-garde linguistic estrangement – as in *Sailor on Land* (*Marinero en tierra*, 1925), by Rafael Alberti, or Lorca's *Gypsy Ballads* – the result is a 'shock' produced by the collision of the old and the new; this is not a return to tradition but a celebration of dislocation. Several poets – including Alberti and Lorca – participated in the 1927 tercentenary of Góngora's death. Góngora's predilection for the violent yoking together of the dissimilar was read by them as anticipating the surrealist concept of metaphor as 'the chance meeting on a dissecting-table of a sewing-machine and an umbrella', to cite Lautréamont's phrase co-opted by the French surrealist André Breton.

The avant-garde's fascination with the modern city was first explored by one of its older members, Ramón Gómez de la Serna (1888–1963), and by a writer dating back to the *fin-de-siècle*, Ramón María del Valle-Inclán (1866–1936). Gómez de la Serna's

1914 *El Rastro* catalogues the disparate objects displayed in Madrid's flea-market of that name, anticipating the surrealist love of the *objet trouvé*. The *flâneur*-narrator relishes his chance encounters with useless objects which defy the capitalist market economy's utilitarian logic. Valle-Inclán's earlier work had exploited the anachronistic juxtaposition of temporalities produced by his modern symbolist rendering of an archaic feudal Galicia. His 1920 play *Bohemian Lights* (*Luces de bohemia*), which elaborates his aesthetic of systematic distortion (*esperpento*), moves to the modern city (Madrid) to experiment with spatial dislocation, with the characters' drunken vision refracted by café mirrors and bisected by street lights. The stage directions anticipate the visual distortions of 1920s German expressionist cinema. Gómez de la Serna would in 1925 construct a fantastic Hollywood in his novel *Cinelandia*. It has been suggested that the experience of the modern city made possible the invention of cinema, for the early motion pictures relied on spectators' visual skills acquired through processing the modern city's rapid, fragmentary, disjointed images. Spanish avant-garde poets avidly attended the 1926–8 film screenings at Madrid's elite university hall of residence, the Residencia de Estudiantes, where Lorca, Dalí, and Buñuel (who chose the films) became friends, followed by those organized 1928–31 by the Spanish Film Club (Cine-Club Español) founded by Giménez Caballero. The preference was for European experimental cinema, which exploited the poetic potential of montage, and for Hollywood silent comedies whose cult of the absurd echoed the surrealist refusal of logic. Alberti's poetic homage to Hollywood comedies – *I Was a Fool and What I Have Seen Has Made Me Two Fools* (*Yo era un tonto y lo que he visto me ha hecho dos tontos*) – was performed by him at a 1929 Spanish Film Club screening. Lorca paid tribute to Hollywood comedies with his dramatic sketch *Buster Keaton's Promenade* (*El paseo de Buster Keaton*, 1928), and while in New York 1929–30 wrote a surrealist film script, *Trip to the Moon* (*Viaje a la luna*), discovered in 1989.

Another cinephile, Francisco Ayala, exploited the modern city's potential in his experimental novella *Hunter at Dawn* (*Cazador en el alba*, 1929), published in the philosopher Ortega y Gasset's *Journal of the West* (*Revista de Occidente*). In his 1926 essay *The Dehumanization of Art* (*La deshumanización del arte*), Ortega had defined modern art as prioritizing style over content and rejecting seriousness for sport. Ayala's novella creates the 'shock of the new' by charting through extravagant metaphor the perceptions of a peasant, Antonio, newly arrived in the city, as he learns to navigate its neon lights and dancing halls. Antonio and his new city girlfriend become efficient machines, not in the sense of dehumanization, but in that they are perfectly synchronized to the city's rhythms which – as in the early cinema of attractions – animate material objects. Antonio becomes a boxer: matter (body) in motion.

Dehumanization of the living and animation of the material coexist in Lorca's *Poet in New York* (*Poeta en Nueva York*, posthumous), written during his 1929–30 stay there. As mentioned in the Introduction, there has been a tendency to back-project Lorca's terrible death onto his work, reading it as necessarily tragic. His poetry is also frequently viewed as the vision of a 'primitive' rural Andalusian alienated in the city. But those who knew him in Madrid describe him as a lynchpin of the urban networking that constituted avant-garde cultural practice. The image of him as rural 'primitive' was not helped by the success of his *Gypsy Ballads*; Lorca had to keep stressing that for him gypsy culture was a way of producing aesthetic effects. Lorca's letters home from New York show him to have been having a terrific time partying with high society and writers of the Harlem Renaissance, with which he coincided. The opposition constructed in his New York poems between the dehumanized world of capitalism – he witnessed the October 1929 Wall Street crash – and the 'primitive', 'natural' world of African-American culture should not be taken to mean that his vision is that of a primitive. The poems' violent metaphors produce a collision of seemingly incompatible worlds – high capitalism, African-American culture – whose coexistence in New York made it, for Lorca, a surrealist city.

Effectively, Lorca's depiction of Harlem's black inhabitants through jungle imagery (monkeys, crocodiles) makes him guilty of primitivism, situating him within the Eurocentric vision that

11. Drawing by Lorca, *Self-Portrait in New York* (*Antorretrato en Nueva York*)

characterizes French surrealism's cult of African art. The Harlem Renaissance's impact on Lorca is felt most strongly in his poems' pulsating rhythms: this was the jazz age. The poem 'Dance of Death' ('Danza de la muerte') takes an African mask to Wall Street. This is not a straightforward opposition between 'natural' African culture and dehumanized American capitalism, for technology too produces a savage energy: 'The primitive beat dances with the mechanical beat' ('El ímpetu primitivo baila con el ímpetu mecánico'). The result is a jazz-like syncopation as two supposedly incompatible rhythms dance together.

Censorship and literary anachronism

During the Franco dictatorship (1939–75), censorship and travel restrictions isolated Spain, particularly in the first two decades. In the mid-1950s, a new generation of 'Angry Young Men' emerged, of whom Juan Goytisolo became the most distinguished. The clandestine political opposition with which these young writers – mostly children of pro-Franco families – sympathized was organized by the illegal Spanish Communist Party. They thus imbibed an orthodox Marxist view of literature as determined by the relations of production, the result being socialist realism (called 'social realism' in Spain for reasons of censorship). Juan Goytisolo later savagely criticized the outmoded espousal of realism by progressive writers (including himself). In fact, most of this mid-1950s protest fiction, when read today, comes over not as realist but as drawing on symbolism to elude censorship – as, for example, in Goytisolo's *Mourning in Paradise* (*Duelo en el Paraíso*, 1955).

In 1962, a literary newcomer, Luis Martín-Santos (1924–64), called realism into question with his Joycean novel *Time of Silence* (*Tiempo de silencio*). To imitate high modernism in the 1960s was also anachronistic. Many writers – politically committed or otherwise – fell silent for several years before coming back with their own experimental fiction. Salient examples are Goytisolo's

Marks of Identity (see Chapter 1), *Day of St. Camillus, 1936* (*San Camilo, 1936*, 1969) by Camilo José Cela (1916–2002), and the Faulknerian *Return to Región* (*Volverás a Región*, 1967) by Juan Benet (1927–93). This new experimentalism was clinched by the mid-1960s triumph of the Latin American novel. Juan Marsé also abandoned realist fiction with *The Fallen* (*Si te dicen que caí*, 1973, banned in Spain till 1976): perhaps the most successful combination of experimental narrative technique with political analysis, achieved by making his child subjects, growing up in a poor district of post-war Barcelona, responsible for the blurring of fantasy and memory.

In the early 1970s, the Barcelona publisher Carlos Barral promoted the 'New Spanish Novel' and the critic José María Castellet published *Nine New Spanish Poets* (*Nueve novísimos poetas españoles*, 1970), launching a cohort of younger writers. The most enduring have been the novelist Javier Marías (1951–), and the poet Pere Gimferrer. Most were marked by a desire, in the Franco dictatorship's closing years, to look ultra-modern and cosmopolitan by sporting a dazzling, promiscuous array of intertextual references to high-cultural sources and English-language pop culture.

Democracy, 'normalization', and the debt to the past

The return to democracy since Franco's death in 1975 has been a 'normalization' process after nearly forty years of dictatorship. Censorship was abolished by the 1978 Constitution. After the virtually obligatory politicization of literature under censorship – for opposition writers, at least – most writers moved to the exploration of personal relationships, such as might be found in any Western country. With the 1982–96 Socialist Government's espousal of neo-liberalism, the publishing industry was subjected to the laws of the global market, several publishers were taken over by multinational consortia (Bertelsmann,

Mondadori). Market logic produced a return to non-experimental fiction, though with a concern for well-crafted prose and an ingenious storyline, often with a thriller component. The bestselling genre has been clever historical fiction: the time-travelling thrillers of Arturo Pérez-Reverte (1951–) plus his Alatriste series set in Spanish Flanders; and the recent successes *The Shadow of the Wind* by Carlos Ruiz Zafón, which uses post-Civil War Barcelona as an exotic backdrop, and *Cathedral of the Sea* by Ildefonso Falcones, which eschews slick literary games for a well-researched recreation of ethnic, class, and gender tensions in medieval Barcelona. At the opposite extreme, the 1990s produced a body of youth-culture fiction, given the American nickname 'Generation X': for example, the postmodern novels of Ray Loriga – *The Worst of All* (*Lo peor de todo*, 1992), *Heroes* (*Héroes*, 1993), and *Fallen from Heaven* (*Caidos del cielo*, 1995) – which recreate the mindset of teenagers whose only reference points are US rock and media culture.

Loriga's *Tokyo Doesn't Love Us Anymore* (*Tokio ya no nos quiere*, 1999) celebrates the freedom afforded by forgetting. In the mid-1980s, a handful of novelists returned to Spain's violent mid-20th-century past. Manuel Vázquez Montalbán combined Communist commitment with the thriller format in his Carvalho series, the most famous being *Murder on the Central Committee* (*Asesinato en el Comité Central*, 1981), while also writing several novels devoted to the Francoist past, of which *The Pianist* (*El pianista*, 1985) graphically evokes former Republicans' struggle for survival. *Wolf Moon* (*Luna de lobos*, 1985) by Julio Llamazares (1955–) poetically explores the gradual expulsion from the community's memory of a group of post-Civil War rural resistance fighters. Llamazares' travel books and his novels *The Yellow Rain* (*La lluvia amarilla*, 1988) and *Scenes from Silent Cinema* (*Escenas de cine mudo*, 1993) recover a rural Spain abandoned through emigration to the city. Antonio Muñoz Molina's *A Manuscript of Ashes* (*Beatus Ille*, 1986) reconstructs the death in the Civil War of a fictitious poet from Lorca's generation – who, in a postmodern twist, turns out to be alive and writing the novel we are reading. Muñoz Molina has taken seriously the ethical duty to remember, particularly in *The Polish Rider (El jinete polaco*, 1991) which explores second-generation 'post-memories' of the Spanish Civil War, *Sepharad (Sefarad*, 2001) which intertwines multiple voices of European Jewish refugees from Nazism, and *The Night of Time (La noche de los tiempos*, 2009) which focuses on a Republican exile.

Since the late 1990s, there has been a 'memory boom' with regard to the Spanish Civil War, which escalated with the bitter public debates accompanying the passage through Congress of the Socialist Government's 2007 law extending the rights of victims of the Civil War and dictatorship (popularly known as 'Historical Memory Law'). The memory boom remains unabated, with practically all Spanish novelists now having produced their Civil War novel – for example, the trilogy *Your Face Tomorrow (Tu rostro mañana*, 2002–7) by Javier Marías, known for well-crafted fiction in which memory triggers exploration of a personal enigma. The most successful fiction on the Civil War has been by relatively new writers. *The Sleeping Voice (La voz dormida*, 2002) by Dulce Chacón (1954–2003) for the first time tackled the plight of former Republican militiawomen in Francoist jails, through a collage of fictitious female voices based on oral-history work with survivors. *The Blind Sunflowers (Los girasoles ciegos*, 2004) by Alberto Méndez (1941–2004), his first and only work, gives a psychologically complex exploration of defeat – resisting the temptation, to which Chacón and most writers succumb, to turn defeat into martyrdom. His four thematically related stories include one about a Francoist soldier who surrenders to the Republican Army shortly before its final defeat, rather than become a victor. Only two other writers have tackled the difficult subject of Francoist supporters. Javier Cercas (1962–), whose phenomenally successful *Soldiers of Salamis (Soldados de Salamina*, 2001) set out to reconstruct the leading fascist intellectual Rafael Sánchez Mazas's real-life escape from a Republican firing squad, comes close to depicting him as a victim, and ducks the issue by veering off into a search for the Republican soldier who saved his life. *The Carpenter's Pencil* (*O lapis do carpinteiro*, 1998, Galician original) by Manuel Rivas (1957–) tells the story of a leading Galician nationalist, jailed and exiled after the Civil War, from a Francoist thug's perspective, acknowledging that Franco's military rebellion was supported by many poor peasants seeking to escape poverty. Although Rivas's depiction of his Galician nationalist protagonist is overly heroic, his novel conveys well how the Francoist repressive apparatus victimized even its henchmen.

That Spanish writers today, to prove their modern democratic credentials, should feel obliged to return to the past is understandable, since politicians and public debate have not done so until very recently. There is a risk, however, of the current literary obsession with the Civil War creating a culture of victimhood, rather than examining the very modern political lessons of the Spanish Republic.

Chapter 3
Gender and sexuality

Since the 1980s, the Spanish literary canon has changed decisively
thanks to the new discipline of gender studies. The result has been
the recovery of 'forgotten' women writers and analysis of literary
representations of femininity, masculinity, and same-sex desire –
often in canonical texts whose gender dimensions had been
ignored. This has not only enlarged the canon but made more
prominent within it writers, particularly women, who seemed less
interesting before gender issues were considered. The
inseparability of the representation of gender from that of sexuality
has also meant new attention to erotic texts previously ignored as
'low' culture, or to erotic aspects overlooked in canonical works.
Texts which illustrate female agency have shot to the top of the
canon. This has irrevocably transformed Golden Age drama:
formerly studied as the expression of Counter-Reformation
theology, it is now much more fun.

Medieval bawdy

Although a major component of European medieval literature,
bawdy has started to be explored in Spanish literature relatively
recently. The divide between high and low culture is a modern
invention, thanks to the Enlightenment's prescription of 'good
taste' as the basis of civility. Like Elizabethan theatre, Golden Age
drama was enjoyed by all social classes. In the Middle Ages,

popular (oral) culture was consumed by the literate and illiterate. The *Book of Good Love* (*Libro de buen amor*, 1330–43) by Juan Ruiz, Archpriest of Hita (1283?–1350?), and Fernando de Rojas's *Celestina* are classic examples of bawdy, mixed with serious genres. This mixture seems shocking today but was not problematic in its time.

One of Ruiz's sources is Medieval Latin Goliardic poetry which, authored by clerical students, celebrates wine, women, and song; Ruiz too was a cleric. His many other sources include sermons, love lyrics, scurrilous songs, proverbs, riddles, *exempla* (some of Arabic origin), the medieval pseudo-Ovidian tradition, debate poetry, and medieval Latin comedy. What most shocks modern readers is Ruiz's enclosure of this literary miscellany in a frame-tale in the form of a first-person account of his many sexual encounters, in which he names himself as the Archpriest of Hita. The 'wildest' episode is his anal penetration by mountain women with prosthetic penises; anal penetration occurs frequently as a form of phallic aggression. Many of the tales, whether involving the narrator or others, have an agonistic quality, typical of popular culture, in which sexual insults – verbal and physical – are traded freely. The mock-epic Battle of Flesh and Lent is a classic carnivalesque celebration of the lower body, in which the ingestion/excretion of food has sexual overtones. The narrator invites readers to distinguish 'good love' from bad, but the mix of profane and religious material leaves critics still unsure what 'good love' means (in fact, the text was given the title *Book of Good Love* only in 1898, by the scholar Ramón Menéndez Pidal).

The procuress (*trotaconventos*) who serves the Archpriest foreshadows the go-between Celestina in Rojas's *Tragicomedy of Calisto and Melibea* (Tragicomedia de Calistoy Melibea). Rojas's work has become known as *Celestina* since she is central to this story of the nobility's destruction by its social inferiors. Earlier critics focused on Melibea's father's final lament, after her suicide on her lover Calisto's death (unheroically falling from a wall), whose elevated humanist tone indicates the text's position on the cusp of the Middle Ages and Renaissance. But that ending is so powerful because it contrasts with the previous reduction of everything to sex, money, and dead bodies. The aristocratic Calisto and Melibea start as courtly lovers but end up using bribes to satisfy their carnal desire. Calisto's servants conspire with Celestina to extort money from him; she convinces the reluctant servant by offering him one of her prostitutes, after warming her up in same-sex foreplay. The two servants stab Celestina to death when she refuses to share her earnings, and are executed. Celestina's speciality is restoring virginities, exposing a sordid underside to the courtly love ideal.

This mix of registers recurs in the Galician-Portuguese love lyric (see Chapter 1). Its genres are the *cantigas de amor* (love songs), *cantigas de amigo* (female-voiced songs addressed to a male lover, written by male authors in poetic 'drag'), and *cantigas d'escarnho e mal dizer* (satirical songs of insult). The same poets

12. Illustration from the 1499 first edition of Fernando de Rojas's *La Celestina*, depicting Celestina's death

wrote in all three styles. As in the *Book of Good Love*, in the scurrilous songs sodomy is a stock means of humiliation.

One of the most outrageous texts is the burlesque poem *Carajicomedia* (literally *Phallocomedy*, 1519, anon.): a 'life and martyrdom' of Diego Fajardo's prick. Its tour of brothels refers explicitly to Celestina, depicting all women as voracious orifices. Diego Fajardo has been identified as the son of Alonso Fajardo, rewarded by the Catholic Monarchs Isabella and Ferdinand for military services in the Conquest of Granada with monopoly ownership of brothels in Andalusia. His son Diego inherited the biggest (notorious) brothel in Málaga. Appropriately, Juan Goytisolo took the title *Carajicomedia* for his 2000 satire of Spanish Catholic moral repression: in his 1970 *Count Julian*, he had subjected the Catholic Queen Isabella – fetishized icon of the Franco Regime – to narrative rape. Goytisolo has repeatedly praised the *Book of Good Love* for its uninhibited carnality.

Mysticism: beyond gender

French feminists, from Simone de Beauvoir's 1949 *The Second Sex* to Luce Irigaray and Hélène Cixous in the 1970s, have explored mysticism as an avenue for female self-expression beyond the masculine/feminine binary. They all single out St Teresa of Avila (1515–82). All three relate mysticism to hysteria, since both allow the possibly liberating loss of a self constrained by patriarchy. Beauvoir more pragmatically argues that the mystic is distinguished from the hysteric by her bodily self-control and influence on the world. What makes Teresa of Avila special is that her mystical ecstasies are accompanied by a project to reform the Carmelite Order.

Mystical discourse describes the soul's union with Christ as a marriage, creating one body which transcends gender distinctions. The soul (feminine in Romance languages) is the Bride of Christ. This places male mystics in the transgendered position of Bride. Irigaray called Christ 'the most feminine of men': this allows female mystics to fuse with a feminized masculine principle that is receptive to femininity. Teresa's writings contain several claims – crossed out by herself or her confessor – that God, unlike men, does not regard women as inferior. Christ's femininity allows the male mystic to bond with it without totally threatening heterosexuality. By contrast, Ramon Llull's 13th-century mystical *Book of the Friend and the Beloved* constructs a male–male union between the mystic and Christ, conceived in terms of homoerotic ideals of male friendship drawn from chivalry and Sufi mysticism.

St John of the Cross (1542–91; beatified 1675, canonized 1726) was spiritual director to the reformed Discalced Carmelite convents founded by Teresa of Avila, for which he was imprisoned by his Carmelite superiors in 1577–8. In prison, he started writing his *Spiritual Canticle* (*Cántico espiritual*, completed 1584), which draws on the biblical *Song of Songs*. In 1572–5, the Inquisition imprisoned the Neoplatonist writer Fray Luis de León for translating the *Song of Songs* from Hebrew (the 1559 Index of Prohibited Books banned vernacular translations of the scriptures). Teresa also wrote a *Meditation on the Song of Songs* in 1566–7, with openly erotic imagery, which she burnt on orders in 1580. St John's assumption of the role of Bride produces a transgendered eroticism grounded in nature imagery. His prose commentaries on his *Spiritual Canticle* have female interlocutors, being written at the request of the Discalced Carmelite nuns he attended.

Teresa of Avila, also writing for the nuns in her reformed Carmelite communities, has been praised for her 'natural' style. However, recent criticism has stressed that she was a consummate strategist, needing to navigate several potential minefields. In the 1940s, it was discovered that her *converso* grandparents and their children (including Teresa's father) had publicly recanted Judaizing practices in a 1485 *auto-de-fé*. Early 16th-century Spain saw the growth of female piety, linked to privately organized *Alumbrado* (Illumined) devotional groups, often under female leadership.

After the Reformation's beginnings in 1517, the *Alumbrados* came under suspicion because of their practice of inner, silent prayer. From 1524, several female *Alumbrado* leaders were tried by the Inquisition for teaching Holy Scripture (forbidden to women). The 1559 Index banned all vernacular guides to devotion. Teresa starts writing in this context, with her *Book of My Life* (*Libro de la Vida*, composed 1562–5) and *Way of Perfection* (*Camino de perfección*, composed c. 1565–9). In 1576, her reformed convents came under attack: in addition to St John of the Cross's incarceration, she was denounced to the Inquisition. The case was dropped but the Carmelite Superior General ordered her reclusion and a ban on founding further reformed convents (both revoked in 1580). She wrote *The Interior Castle* (*Las moradas del castillo interior*) in 1577. In 1579, several female *Alumbrados* were condemned in an *auto-de-fé* for reporting erotic visions of Christ, seen as a cover for sexual orgies. This made ecstatic trances, such as Teresa had claimed, intensely suspect. Teresa's *Book of Foundations* was written 1573–82.

Fray Luis de León published her works in 1588, six years after her death. From 1589 to 1591, an Inquisitorial prosecutor tried to get her books burned. When her *Life* passed from the Inquisition to Philip II's Escorial library, he initiated proceedings to have her declared patron saint of the Spanish Crown. She was beatified in 1614 and canonized in 1622 (the only woman canonized during the Counter-Reformation). Her nomination as co-patron saint of Spain (with the previous incumbent, St James 'the Moor-slayer') was ratified by Pope Urban VIII in 1627, almost immediately revoked, and reconfirmed by the Spanish liberal parliament besieged in Cadiz by Napoleon's troops in 1812. General Franco 'captured' her hand from a Republican colonel (supposedly in a suitcase full of banknotes) in 1937 and kept it at his El Pardo residence throughout his life; it accompanied him during his prolonged death in 1975 – a horrible irony for a woman who spent most of her life trying to negotiate her way round opposition from her male Church superiors.

Teresa was thus writing with the constant possibility of falling out of favour, not unlike Baroque courtiers who had to manufacture a fictitious persona. She persisted with her reform programme, founding convents without endowments so they would not depend on powerful donors who expected the nuns to spend their time praying for their salvation. This allowed her to admit nuns of all social classes (several girls ran away from home to join) and for them to devote themselves to mental prayer – a practice which, although pursued by the Inquisition, she never abandoned. To achieve this, in her writings she protested feminine weakness and ignorance, and stressed her dependence on her male confessors (one, at least, was supportive). Her *Life* was written on her confessor's orders to defend her mystical visions and practice of mental prayer against possible accusations of heresy – much as the picaresque novel's first-person narrators address their life-stories to an authority figure. Her autobiography is, literally, a confession. Her use of contradiction and paradox prevents critics from pinning her down. Her *Way of Perfection* and *Interior Castle* were explicitly written to satisfy her nuns' request for spiritual guidance; her use of 'women's language', without erudite biblical quotation, helped avoid accusations of teaching the scriptures in the vernacular and, indeed, of teaching the scriptures as a woman. The manuscripts of her work show the substantial revisions she and her confessors made to ensure at least nominal orthodoxy. She has been called 'virile' for her foundational enterprises; alternatively, one could say that she used feminine wiles strategically to get what she wanted.

Resourceful early modern women

Not normally included in the canon are a number of picaresque novels with female protagonists – whores whose servicing of multiple clients allows exposure of social hypocrisy. The detailed descriptions of sexual activity show that these texts also had an erotic function. The best known, *The Lusty Andalusian Woman* (*La lozana andaluza*, 1528) by Francisco Delicado (c. 1480 to after

1534), precedes *Lazarillo* and is explicitly indebted to *Celestina*, whose dialogue-form it adopts. In a modern touch, the 'author' includes himself as a character, introducing himself to his protagonist Lozana as the writer of her life-story and giving his biographical details (they are both Cordobans living in Rome). This makes the author, and the reader with him, a voyeur witnessing what Lozana gets up to in private. The author's first-hand knowledge of Rome's sexual underworld – which biographical evidence suggests was real – makes his narrative simultaneously reliable (testimonial) and unreliable (morally dubious). The text's various afterwords include one from Lozana reporting the 1527 Sack of Rome by Charles V's imperial troops, presented as punishment for the city's sins – but she ends by saying she would otherwise happily have continued as before.

Delicado is writing before the Counter-Reformation. From the mid-16th century, there was increased regulation and enclosure of prostitutes, whether in licensed brothels or Magdalen houses – another parallel with late 19th-century Spain (see Chapter 2). Consequently, later female picaresque novels are more misogynist. Only *La pícara Justina* (1605), by Francisco López de Úbeda (n.d.), allows its female protagonist to give a first-person account; the rest are 'spoken for' by the male narrators. The protagonist of *Celestina's Daughter* (*La hija de la Celestina*, 1612), by Alonso Jerónimo de Salas Barbadillo (1581–1635), is garrotted and thrown into the river in a barrel.

The autobiography of Catalina de Erauso (1592–1650), *The Story of the Lieutenant-Nun* (*Historia de la monja alférez*, written c. 1624–5), has attracted much attention. In its day, her story circulated in broadsides and a play, and has since attracted numerous adaptations, including films and comics. From an aristocratic Basque family, at the age of 15 Catalina ran away from the convent where she was being educated and lived as a man fighting on the Chilean and Peruvian colonial frontier for almost 20 years till, to escape prosecution for murder, she confessed to being a woman. Returning to Spain in 1624 as a celebrity, she obtained a royal pension for her military services and papal dispensation to continue to dress as a man (which she did, returning to Mexico in 1630). Various factors contributed to the lack of censure: the contemporary vogue for cross-dressing in the theatre (see below); the taste for 'freaks' in popular broadsides; the fact that medical examination proved she was a virgin; and her insistence on her patriotic motives (there were other cases of women rewarded for fighting as men in Spain's army in Europe). No one, it seems, was disturbed by her life of brawling as a soldier (in the course of which she killed some dozen men, including her brother). Even the priest who took her confession in Lima was unconcerned by her occasional homoerotic dalliances with women who thought she was a man, since there was no genital activity. Her autobiography mimics the picaresque genre; it is also an example of the Baroque aesthetic, founded on disguise and sensational effects. The 1626 play *The Lieutenant-Nun* (*La monja alférez*) by Juan Pérez de Montalbán (1602–38) ignores her military exploits for a comic intrigue in which a woman falls in love with her in her male disguise – a standard plot device in contemporary cross-dressing comedies.

Cross-dressing occurs in several interpolated stories in *Don Quixote*. Both Dorotea and the Morisca Ana Félix are admired for dressing as a man to pursue their goals. Cervantes' tolerant attitude towards his female characters – defending their right to marry (or not) as they please – is widely recognized. Male-to-female cross-dressing occurs in Cervantes' work only in the context of Ottoman Algiers: Ana Félix dresses her Christian lover as a woman to save him from 'inevitable' sodomization. There have been attempts to 'queer' Cervantes on the assumption that he 'must' have had homosexual experiences during his captivity in Algiers, but there is no evidence. The gender fluidity produced by cross-dressing in Golden Age literature is likely to have nothing to do with homosexuality. Rather, it illustrates the pre-Enlightenment concept of gender as a continuum rather than a binary opposition: women were regarded as less developed members of the human species than men, but not as essentially different (as would become the case from the late 18th century).

Male-to-female cross-dressing is relatively infrequent in Golden Age literature, partly because it was much more worried by effeminate men than by manly women, and also because in Spain, unlike Elizabethan England, actresses were allowed on stage, so there is no theatrical convention of boys acting female roles. Female-to-male cross-dressing is, however, incredibly common. The manly woman (*mujer varonil*) was a stock dramatic theme. At least one new play with a manly woman protagonist was produced every year from 1590 to 1660; around 150 such plays have been counted. Not all manly woman plays include cross-dressing, and many plays involving cross-dressing do not feature manly women: for example, Tirso de Molina's romp *Don Gil with the Green Breeches* (*Don Gil de las Calzas Verdes*, 1615). Some plays – like *La monja alférez* – were written for actresses who specialized in cross-dressing roles; one of these, Bárbara Coronel, wore male clothes offstage. Practically all these plays end with the manly woman capitulating to marriage: there is no serious disturbance to gender roles, but there is a lot of fun and Baroque play with appearances, and in the process women's roles are greatly expanded.

Only one dramatic heroine rejects men because she desires a woman: Dionisia in *Añasco from Talavera* (*Añasco el de Talavera*, n.d.) by Álvaro Cubillo de Aragón (c. 1596–1661); she too finally marries. Lope de Vega established the manly woman convention in the 1590s and remained its greatest exponent. The most popular category of manly woman was the *mujer esquiva* who spurns men and marriage, as in the Elizabethan 'taming of the shrew' theme. Next in popularity were female bandits or soldiers, female huntresses, and scholarly women (in that order). Many *mujeres esquivas* are resisting a forced marriage: for example, Tirso's *Martha the Pious* (*Marta la piadosa*, 1614–15) whose heroine fakes a religious vocation, acquiring self-determination through deceit.

All dramatists condemn forced marriages, which were forbidden by a 1567 decree. It is, however, assumed that it is natural for women to marry. Several plays – such as Calderón's *No Trifling with Love* (*No hay burlas con el amor*, 1635?) – have disdainful heroines who, as in Shakespeare's *Much Ado about Nothing*, are won over by suitors who feign indifference. Uppity women also get their comeuppance in plays about bluestockings. Unlettered women triumph over learned sisters in Lope's *The Simple-Minded Lady* (*La dama boba*, 1613) and *Outwardly Simple-Minded, Inwardly Discreet* (*La boba para los otros y discreta para sí*, 1623–35). However, in *Medical Love* (*El amor médico*, 1618–25?), Tirso is sympathetic to his heroine who, disguised as a man, wins a university chair and becomes court physician. Although, when she finally marries, she gives up her career, there is no suggestion she will abandon her books.

Female bandits are always treated sympathetically, provided they revert to docile femininity at the end. Lope is the dramatist most worried by clever women but the most generous to his female bandits. The bandits with the worst crimes are sometimes pretexts to demonstrate God's mercy, as in Calderón's *Devotion of the Cross* (*La devoción de la cruz*, c. 1633), and Tirso's *Bandit Countess or the Heavenly Nymph* (*La condesa bandolera o la ninfa del cielo*, 1613), whose man-slayer heroine is at the end carried up to heaven by Christ. But most female-bandit plays explore the problem of women shunned by society because they have been dishonoured – the usual reason why they take to the hills. *Valour, Insult and Woman* (*Valor, agravio y mujer*, n.d.) by the female dramatist Ana Caro (1590–1650) is not a bandit drama, but her heroine Leonor cross-dresses to pursue the man who has dishonoured her (called Don Juan, in a likely riposte to Tirso's seducer hero) all the way to Flanders, where the woman he is courting falls in love with her in her male disguise. She gets Don Juan to the altar. There were frequent attempts to regulate or ban female cross-dressing on stage, but none succeeded; Lope noted that this dramatic device never failed to please. A major attraction was the sight of actresses' thighs in tight hose. But the cross-dressing and manly woman plots also exposed audiences to a range of unorthodox female behaviour which was clearly enjoyed, even if the main pleasure may have consisted in seeing errant women submit to husbands at the end.

The one bestselling woman author in early 17th-century Spain was María de Zayas (1590–1661), whose two novella collections, *Exemplary Love Stories* (*Novelas amorosas y ejemplares*, 1637) and *Disenchantments of Love* (*Desengaños amorosos*, 1647), built on the popularity of Cervantes' *Exemplary Novels* (*Novelas ejemplares*, 1613). Like Cervantes, Zayas draws on the framed-tale convention, via Boccaccio; if Cervantes innovated by dispensing with the narrative frame, Zayas makes the frame into a story in itself. In the first volume, a group of female and male courtiers meets to amuse the sick Lisis, jilted by her lover, each telling a tale on successive nights. In the second volume, they reconvene to celebrate Lisis's engagement to a new lover. Now only women may tell stories, which must all illustrate disenchantment with love – after the last story, Lisis breaks off her engagement and retires to a convent. Zayas abandons the usual happy end: only two stories end with the initial couple marrying; two end with the male protagonist's death; most end with the heroines renouncing the world; and the second volume contains a horrific amount of domestic violence (often fatal) against women. There is rape, torture, mutilation, male and female cross-dressing, lesbian desire, male homosexuality (one wife has to witness her husband in bed with his page). The courtiers are required to tell 'true' stories, but this is the sensational, gory 'truth' of contemporary broadsides, seamlessly mixing popular and courtly culture. Zayas's work was not censored, perhaps thanks to her narrative equivocations. Lisis, especially, bends over backwards to point out women's defects, while insisting that the storytelling sessions' goal is to counter male slanders of her sex. Both men and women deceive: men make false promises of marriage, while women have a phenomenal capacity for dissimulation or disguise – this makes the women, rather than the men, accomplished examples of Baroque self-fashioning through fiction.

Zayas's stories are also fascinated with the abject, sometimes racially inflected. In the autobiographical story told by Lisis's Moorish slave Zelima, the latter turns out to be a Christian who, raped and abandoned, marked her face with (fake) slave-branding and had herself sold into slavery. In another story, a wife, slandered by her black female slave, is reduced to abjection by her husband; in another, a black male slave is reduced to abjection by the sexual demands of his white mistress. Zayas's work invites a psychoanalytic reading.

Women and social control: 17th- and 19th-century parallels

We have seen how both early modern and late 19th-century Spain were concerned with the control of vagrants and prostitutes. This section explores anxieties common to both periods about the control of women, and especially about female adultery. There are different underlying master-narratives: in early modern Spain, blood purity; in Restoration Spain, erosion of the public/private boundary. But in both these periods of nation-formation, wives become the 'trouble in the text'. The texts concerned are late 16th- and early 17th-century honour dramas (known as 'wife-murder' plays) and the 1880s realist novel.

In both periods, husbands were legally entitled to kill adulterous wives and their lovers (this changed only with the 1932 Republican divorce law). Male adultery was not a criminal offence. Research suggests that husbands rarely exercised their murderous prerogative in either period; the literary recurrence of female adultery relates to wider anxieties. Fourteen wife-murder plays by Lope have been counted, seven by Calderón, two by Tirso, and twelve by other playwrights. Female adultery is the topic of six novels of Galdós (excluding his historical novels), one by Pardo Bazán (see below), and both novels of Alas.

In Golden Age honour dramas, wives are killed almost always for suspicion of adultery – as, for example, in Calderón's best-known wife-murder plays, *The Surgeon of His Honour* (*El médico de su honra*, 1929), *Secret Injury, Secret Vengeance* (*A secreto agravio secreta venganza*, 1635), and *The Painter of His Dishonour* (*El pintor de su deshonra*, 1640–50). Lope's *Punishment without Revenge* (*El castigo sin venganza*, 1631) is an exceptional case of actual adultery. The fact that the key issue is suspicion corroborates recent readings of these plays as dramas of legibility, related to contemporary obsessions about blood purity – disturbing since it could not be 'read on the body'. Hence the Inquisition's sophisticated interrogation techniques. Wife-murder plays became increasingly popular in the early 17th century, at the moment when policy towards the Moriscos changed from integration to expulsion. There is a similar shift in writing about wives. The 16th-century corpus of conduct manuals, of which the best known is Fray Luis de León's 1583 *The Perfect Wife* (*La perfecta casada*), supposes that wives can perfect themselves but criticizes them for bettering their appearance with cosmetics, since this makes it hard to 'read' what they 'really are'. In the wife-murder plays, mostly written in the early 17th century, the husband takes it for granted that his wife is 'tainted'; the issue is how to 'read' the 'stain' on her body. As with the Inquisition's torture procedures, the husband pushes his inquiry till he gets the result he is looking for. This was explicitly critiqued in Cervantes' interpolated story 'Impertinent Curiosity' (*'El curioso impertinente'*) in the *Quixote*: the jealous husband hires a friend to 'test' his wife and, when the tests prove negative, insists he persevere until the inevitable happens. The early 17th century was the time when blood purity statutes started to be called into question. The wife-murder plays are today read as an illustration of that questioning, or at least of the anxieties produced by an inquisitorial mentality that generated constant suspicion.

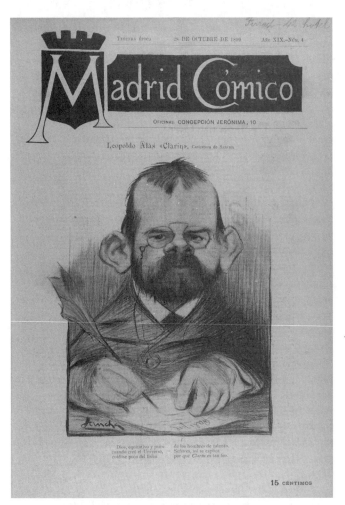

13. Cartoon of Leopoldo Alas ('Clarín') on the cover of *Madrid Cómico* (28 October 1899)

The mid-to-late 19th century also produced a corpus of female conduct manuals, now written by the new medical experts to whom Foucault attributed the modern 'surveillance society'. In the realist novel, female adultery takes place in the city, where social control and consumerism produce a two-way erosion of the public/private boundary as social improvers invade the home and women go out shopping. Galdós, as we have seen, is the great novelist of consumerism. Alas's *La Regenta* depicts the invasion of the marital home by traditional and modern improvers (a priest, a politician, and a doctor). Post-Enlightenment medicine saw men and women as radically different since their reproductive organs supposedly determined their entire being. This justified the continuing confinement of women to the home, despite the liberal doctrine of universal rights, since women were made for motherhood. Alas's protagonist Ana is childless since her older husband Víctor is sexually ineffective. The only man who has regular (non-sexual) access to her body is her highly professionalized doctor. The two intruders into her home who want to bed her are her confessor, Fermín – the only man in Vetusta (a fictionalized version of Oviedo) sensitive enough to understand her but a power-seeker who uses the confessional to gain influence – and the local Liberal Party leader, Álvaro – a Don Juan who seduces women to enhance his political charisma. Worries about confessors' influence on women were strong at the time; Alas's journalism combats the violation of individual rights produced by state centralization. Ana is literally married to the law ('La Regenta' means 'The Judge's Wife'): extraordinarily, Víctor, on discovering that his wife has succumbed to Álvaro, does not 'judge' her, understanding that her young body needs sexual fulfilment. Alas's narrator, however, is another intruder into Ana's privacy who constructs her inner life – largely narrated via reported interior monologue – through the lens of modern medicine's pathologization of female psychology. No doubt for this reason, the narrator does not depict Ana's doctor's invasion of her privacy as a threat.

14. Still from Spanish state television's serialization of *La Regenta* (directed by Fernando Méndez Leite, 1994–5)

Emilia Pardo Bazán (1851–1921) was a political conservative partly because she realized the liberal public/private division had made things worse for women. Her gender critique is radical. In *The House of Ulloa* (*Los pazos de Ulloa*, 1886), Nucha is physically abused by her rural landowner husband, not just on false suspicion of adultery with the manor's chaplain, but because she has given birth to a girl instead of the desired male heir. The novel unhinges maternity from biology, making Nucha, physically unsuited to childbirth, the perfect mother, and depicting the effeminate chaplain Julián as a second mother to Nucha's daughter. The sequel *Mother Nature* (*La madre naturaleza*, 1887) narrates the unwitting incest of Nucha's daughter Manuela, left to run wild after her mother's death, with her illegitimate half-brother Perucho, unrecognized by their father. Perucho is Manuela's nurse, mother, father, and brother, as he says. Their relationship is 'fraternal' in that it is based on complete equality. The novel critiques Rousseau's *Émile*, which advocated a natural education for boys but confined girls to home-making. Nucha's brother Gabriel decides to 'save' the adolescent Manuela by claiming her as his wife. But Manuela, thanks to her natural education, outwits his attempts as Rousseauesque tutor to 'domesticate' her. When Manuela and Perucho, after making love, are told they are half-brother and sister, the three male social controllers – Gabriel (would-be husband), Julián (Church), and the atheist doctor (medicine) – gather at Manuela's bedside. Manuela refuses marriage to Gabriel, and agrees to go into a convent only temporarily so Perucho can return to claim his position as heir. Pardo Bazán was a devout Catholic, though sexually unorthodox (she separated from her husband because he opposed her writing and in the late 1880s had an affair with Galdós). The novel offers no censure of Manuela and Perucho's adolescent sexual intercourse.

In 1892, Pardo Bazán created a 'Women's Library' (Biblioteca de la Mujer), whose publications included María de Zayas's novellas, August Bebel's *Woman under Socialism*, and J. S. Mill's *The*

15. **Emilia Pardo Bazán, 1918 (reproduced on the cover of the newspaper *ABC*'s commemorative edition on her death in 1921)**

Subjection of Women, which she translated herself as *La esclavitud de la mujer* (*The Enslavement of Women*).

Melodrama and feminine sensibility

Melodrama's emotional excess is usually regarded as in bad taste. Modern critics have justified it since it forces readers or theatre-goers to confront unacceptable emotions. The genre's predilection for female victims has been used strategically by female writers to convey a female subjectivity grounded in repression.

Gertrudis Gómez de Avellaneda's *Sab* (1841), the first Spanish-language anti-slavery novel, anticipates *Uncle Tom's Cabin* by ten years. Gómez de Avellaneda (1814–73) moved from Cuba to Spain aged 22. The novel uses melodramatic conventions to portray not only the subordination of women in colonial Cuba but also the mulatto slave Sab's hopeless love for his master's daughter, Carlota. Western culture has frequently depicted other cultures as feminine. Here that equation produces empathy with Sab for being denied a 'manly' status, while showing his feminine sensibility to be superior to the calculating rationalism of bourgeois white males like Carlota's English merchant fiancé. Sab outdoes the female characters in his capacity for self-sacrifice; his 'femininity' is what makes him deserving. It also dooms him to die.

The conventions of melodrama are pushed to the limit in Rosalía de Castro's 1859 novel *The Daughter of the Sea* (*La hija del mar*) which explores mother–daughter relationships: those of Esperanza with her adoptive mother Teresa and her biological mother Candora from whom she was snatched as a baby. Esperanza, brought by the sea at the novel's start, leaps into it to die at the end. The sea is an image of unpredictability (storms mirror the female characters' emotions) and of loss (the three women spend much of the novel wandering the coastline vainly searching for each other). Their separation is caused by the novel's villain, Alberto, who, having seduced and abandoned Candora, seduces and abandons Teresa, returning to lock her and Esperanza up in his villa. The marital home is a prison. The melodramatic reliance on coincidence disrupts time and space: the jumps between chapters leave us disoriented. The novel's structure illustrates what Julia Kristeva called 'women's time': discontinuous and cyclical, like the motion of the sea.

By contrast, Carmen de Burgos (1867–1932) put melodramatic conventions to political use. Her press campaigns for a divorce law included stories (written 1907–25) for cheap, serialized novella collections aimed at a broad readership. Melodrama's reliance on innocent heroines and male villains is mobilized to dramatize terrible fates awaiting wives unable to exit marriage. *Article 438* (*El artículo 438*, 1921), named after the Penal Code article permitting husbands to kill unfaithful wives, depicts a wife murdered by a spendthrift husband when, during one of his many absences, she strikes up a caring relationship with another man. This gives the husband the excuse he wanted to kill her so he can inherit her wealth. Burgos, whose own personal life was unconventional, supported herself as a journalist. In her work, the clear-cut morality of melodrama becomes a refusal to compromise. The official commentary on the Spanish Republic's 1932 Divorce Law, passed the year she died, recognized her as a pioneer.

In 1945, Carmen Laforet (1921–2004) won the newly created Nadal Prize with a first novel, *Nothing* (*Nada*), depicting a dysfunctional right-wing family, ruined by the Civil War, through the eyes of its first-person narrator, Andrea, newly arrived in Barcelona to study at university. The melodramatic emotions are those of the family she observes, whose latent hysteria simmers throughout. In a gender reversal, the hysterics are the males: Román, a perversely seductive black-marketeer tortured during the Civil War for being a Francoist spy; and the mentally unstable Juan, who beats his working-class wife (the household's breadwinner). There is a feminine melodramatic strand in the abject story of Margarita, the mother of Andrea's wealthy university friend, Ena. When young, Margarita had cut off her plait in a sacrificial act designed to win Román's love; he mocked her. The pent-up emotions in both families come together explosively when Ena, to avenge her mother, seduces Román and laughs in his face. Román slits his throat. It was illegal to mention suicide in 1945; how the novel escaped the early Franco dictatorship's stringent censorship has never been explained.

Masculine anxieties

Representations of masculinity in Spanish literature are understudied. Excellent work has been done on *La Regenta*, exploring the complex psychological make-up of the novel's male protagonist, the priest Fermín – arguably better drawn than that of the heroine Ana. The key to Fermín's contradictory personality is his inability to separate from his domineering mother. Psychoanalytic exploration of Unamuno's literary output has also been productive, though it has not totally broken with standard views of his fictional experimentalism as the expression of a gender-neutral existential angst. His representation of women has been seen as illustrating his hostility to contemporary feminist debate. But his literary works reveal not so much an unreflective misogyny as a very self-aware exploration of masculine anxiety.

His most experimental novel, *Fog* (*Niebla*, 1914), explores its protagonist Augusto's angst on discovering that he is Unamuno's fictional character, but dramatizes his insecurity specifically in relation to women. We might further ask what Unamuno's insistence on flaunting his authorial control over Augusto tells us about male–male relationships; fear of other males is dramatized in several of Unamuno's works, such as his play *The Other* (*El otro*, 1926). Augusto's insecurity is explicitly linked to his dependence on his recently deceased mother. Male anxieties about mothers are explored in the story *Two Mothers* (*Dos madres*, one of Unamuno's *Tres novelas ejemplares*, 1920) and the novel *Aunt Tula* (*La tía Tula*, 1921), both about women who push men into fathering children with other women so they can appropriate the children themselves, while refusing to marry. This reveals male anxieties about women who reject marital subservience to men, but also about male proprietorship of children. In Spain, virility has traditionally been measured by the number of children a man fathers, and the law gave women no custodial rights over their children – something that divorce campaigners were challenging.

Unamuno's most complex exploration of masculine anxiety is *Abel Sánchez* (1917). In 1946, Carlos Serrano de Osma brilliantly filmed the novel through the lens of Hollywood *film noir*, a genre seen as exploring a split male ego, embodied in the dual attraction to a *femme fatale* and a safe, nurturing woman. This is the plot of *Abel Sánchez*. The parts of the film dialogue that explicitly address sexual anxieties are taken verbatim from the novel. The Franco dictatorship packaged Unamuno as a puritanical author obsessed with 'the problem of Spain'. He is equally obsessed with masculinity.

Another fictional expression of masculine anxiety is Cela's *The Family of Pascual Duarte* (*La familia de Pascual Duarte*, 1942). Critics eager to find signs of opposition culture in early Francoist Spain read the novel as social critique. But its peasant serial killer is clearly depicted as driven by his fear of not being seen as a 'proper man'. Male sexuality is the theme of all Cela's work – often depicted in a way that offends female readers.

I end this section with a novel by Rosa Chacel which ostensibly explores female identity: *Memoirs of Leticia Valle* (*Memorias de Leticia Valle*, 1945), written in exile in Argentina. The precocious 11-year-old who narrates her story repudiates domestic femininity and develops an attachment to the local archivist Daniel and his artistic wife Julia. This starts with her same-sex desire for Julia, but develops into a desire to 'conquer' Daniel. She does this by mimicking masculinity, engaging in a male–male battle of wills which drives Daniel to suicide. Chacel, a protégée of Ortega y Gasset, was one of the first Spaniards to read Freud, whose work was, thanks to Ortega, translated into Spanish 1922–34 (the first translation of Freud's collected works into any language). Freud, who never managed to move from his analysis of the male Oedipus complex to a version that worked for girls, ended up suggesting that the little girl replaced her desire to be the father with a desire to have a baby by him. Chacel's Leticia wants to be the father.

Claiming female experience

If Rosalía de Castro founded modern Galician literature, women writers have been important also in 20th-century Catalan literature. The novel *Solitude* (*Solitud*, 1905) by Caterina Albert (1869–1966, pen-name Víctor Català) contributes to Catalan *modernisme*'s symbolist vision, using its isolated Pyrenean backdrop to express mood. It traces its female protagonist Mila's developing self-awareness, thanks to the semi-mythical shepherd who tells her fairytales and guides her to the mountain peaks, and the spirit of evil Ànima (nothing to do with Jungian archetypes) who rapes her, teaching her she can survive anything.

Like Albert, the best-known Catalan woman writer, Mercè Rodoreda, published several short-story collections. Her 1962 novel, *The Time of the Doves* (*La plaça del Diamant*, 1962), written in exile in Geneva, is notable for exploring working-class female subjectivity. The first-person narrator-protagonist, Natàlia, unable to express her emotions, conveys them indirectly through her relationship to the material objects in her life – the most important of which is the dovecote her husband Quimet builds on their terrace. Far from a symbol of peace, the doves represent Quimet's invasion of her interiority and her home's invasion by the Civil War, which leaves her a widow. The depiction of sexuality is complex: Natàlia's highly physical relationship with Quimet subjects her to him; she finds contentment with her second husband, impotent from a war wound but caring.

Albert and Rodoreda were not writing within a feminist tradition. The later Montserrat Roig (1946–91) and Carme Riera (1948–) self-consciously explore female identity while recognizing its elusiveness. Roig started writing in the late 1960s at a time of increasing left-wing activism; her journalism focused on women's issues. Her novels depict a fragmented female consciousness, situating her female characters historically. The trilogy *Goodbye*

Ramona (*Ramona, adéu,* 1972), *The Time of the Cherries* (*El temps de les cireres,* 1977), and *The Violet Hour* (*L'hora violeta,* 1980) depicts women's lives in two Barcelona families since the late 19th century, constructing a female genealogy. Her female characters express themselves through writing (letters, diaries, journalism, fiction) and photography. The last novel includes the novel-within-the-novel that Natàlia has asked a female friend to write about her mother's passionate Civil War relationship with a Republican militiawoman, representing a lost possibility of female emancipation (the Republic gave women the vote as well as divorce; the Franco dictatorship revoked all women's rights). Roig shows how male anti-Franco militants internalized patriarchal attitudes.

Riera started to publish the year Franco died (1975), co-founding Spain's first feminist magazine, *Feminist Defence* (*Vindicación Feminista*) (1976–9). The transition to democracy allowed feminist activism, previously subsumed under the anti-Franco struggle, to develop independently. Riera's fiction conveys female subjectivity through complex narrative techniques (she is a Professor of Spanish Literature). Her early stories 'I Leave You, My Love, the Sea as a Token' ('Te deix, amor, la mar com a penyora', 1975) and 'I Call on the Seagulls as Witness' ('Jo pos per testimoni les gavines', 1977) explore lesbian desire. The first – a passionate female love letter – makes readers confront their heterosexist assumptions by finally revealing that the addressee is a woman. The second – a letter to Riera from the 'real-life' recipient of the earlier story's letter – gives lesbianism a testimonial dimension. Riera's later work does not treat lesbian desire but continues to explore female intimacy as a way of seducing the reader. She has also turned to the historical novel to make reparation to her native Majorca's substantial *converso* community. Her prize-winning *In the Last Blue* (*Dins el darrer blau,* 1994) allows the 37 *conversos* burnt by the Inquisition in 1691 to tell their stories in their own voice. However, the focus on their private lives, while giving attention to women, risks eclipsing the event's political dimensions. The later novel *Towards the Open Sky* (*Cap el cel obert*, 2000) depicts prejudice against a Majorcan woman of Jewish descent in 1850s Havana.

In the Basque Country, women writers did not come to the fore until the mid-1990s, the most successful being Laura Mintegi (1955–), whose novel *Nerea and I* (*Nerea eta biok*, 1994; Spanish translation *Nerea y yo*) explores women's role in relation to Basque nationalism. It was also in the 1990s that Castilian-language women writers achieved equal status with their male peers; since then, their work has sold well. The recovery of past women writers began in the 1980s, largely thanks to US feminist scholars. The most dramatic 'recovery' was that of María Martínez Sierra (1874–1974), who published her five books of feminist essays (1916–32) and a prolific dramatic output under the name of her cultural impresario husband, Gregorio Martínez Sierra. This seems to have been a strategic decision: feigned male authorship allowed her to be more outspoken in promoting women's rights. Her essays stress the importance of education and work for women, advocating a feminine ethics of care. From 1930, she devoted herself to Socialist political activism, winning a parliamentary seat at the 1933 elections, the first in which women voted. In 1952, in exile in Argentina, she published under her own name her autobiographical account of her Socialist campaigning, *A Woman on the Road in Spain* (*Una mujer por los caminos de España*).

A number of women writers of the 1920s and 1930s, when Madrid's literary circles were sexually emancipated, became virtually forgotten in exile after the Civil War, overshadowed by their writer husbands: Concha Méndez (1898–1986), married to Manuel Altolaguirre; Ernestina de Champourcin (1905–99), married to Juan José Domenchina (all poets); and María Teresa León (1903–88), wife of poet and dramatist Rafael Alberti. León introduced Alberti to communist activism and played a major role in the Republic's wartime cultural programme (see Chapter 4).

Her autobiography *Memoir of Melancholy* (*Memoria de la melancolía*, 1970), written in exile, has become a classic of Spanish women's literature. Its fluctuation between first, second, and third person highlights the instability of female identity, aggravated by the dislocation of exile. As with María Martínez Sierra, autobiography has been important for female exile writers as a way to reclaim their voice.

Two women novelists married to famous writer husbands in the 1950s to 1960s – Carmen Martín Gaite (1925–2000), wife of Rafael Sánchez Ferlosio, and Josefina Aldecoa (1926–), wife of Ignacio Aldecoa – have flourished since the return to democracy, eclipsing their former husbands. Martín Gaite's early fiction (1957–76) highlights women's need for an interlocutor in order to establish a sense of identity. This 'feminist' orientation (a label she rejected) blossomed from 1978, when she won Spain's National Fiction Prize with *The Back Room* (*El cuarto de atrás*, 1978). The novel is a memory trip back to her Francoist girlhood, prompted by a mysterious male muse (an inversion of the usual 'woman as muse' trope) who disorders her memories so they can be released from the 'back room' of her mind. The material recovered forms the basis of her later historical study *Courtship Customs in Postwar Spain* (*Usos amorosos en la posguerra española*, 1981). Her subsequent novels develop this exploration of memory as the basis of identity, through the re-establishment of girlhood friendship in *Variable Cloud* (*Nubosidad variable*, 1992) and of contact with mothers by the male protagonist of *The Snow Queen* (*La Reina de las Nieves*, 1994) and the female protagonists of *Living's the Strange Thing* (*Lo raro es vivir*, 1996) and *Leaving Home* (*Irse de casa*, 1998). In all these novels, memories teach the protagonists that they are bound up with the lives of others.

After a 1961 short-story collection, Aldecoa stopped publishing till 1983. Her trilogy *Story of a Schoolteacher* (*Historia de una maestra*, 1990), *Women in Black* (*Mujeres de negro*, 1994), and *The Force of Destiny* (*La fuerza del destino*, 1997) established her as a major writer, again expressing female subjectivity through memory. The first novel is a minimalist masterpiece as Gabriela writes, for her daughter Juana, her account of her experiences as a village schoolteacher in 1920s Equatorial Guinea and then under the Republic in north-west Spain, where her husband is killed during the 1934 Asturian Miners' Strike (whose repression by General Franco was a rehearsal for the Civil War). The second novel switches to Juana's narration of Gabriela's exile in Mexico and her own return to study in Madrid in the 1950s, where she participates in the first anti-Franco student demonstrations (like Roig, she notes the Spanish Left's *machismo*). The last novel reverts to Gabriela's narrative voice as she returns, on Franco's death, to a Spain no longer her own. While privileging the mother–daughter relationship, the trilogy shows the private to be inscribed in history.

Women who started writing after the return to democracy have embraced the market with notable success. Most have opted for realist depiction of the vertiginous social changes undergone by women since 1975. Spain's record for the number of women in top professional positions today is impressive; since its 2004 election victory, the current Socialist Government has appointed women to at least 50% of Cabinet positions; women have outnumbered men at university since 1990. Rosa Montero (1951–), a top columnist for Spain's major newspaper *El País*, has written popular novels about working women's problems with men who have not adapted to female emancipation, breaking taboos on discussing issues such as female orgasm, masturbation, and menstruation. The younger Lucía Etxebarría (1966–) has cultivated a *risqué* image attuned to youth culture (sex, drugs, and rock'n'roll) while exploring different models of femininity – including bisexuality and lesbianism in *Beatrice and the Heavenly Bodies* (*Beatriz y los cuerpos celestes*, 1998). She has been criticized for playing the market and admired for brazenly exposing its workings. Almudena Grandes (1960–) achieved notoriety with her first novel *The Ages of Lulu* (*Las edades de Lulú*, 1989), written for a cult pornography series, which nevertheless ends with its heroine being rescued from a heavy S&M scenario by her husband, who tucks her up in bed dressed in baby clothes. Grandes has since developed into an impressive, if conventionally realist, writer: *Malena is a Tango Name* (*Malena es un nombre de tango*, 1994) is a female *Bildungsroman*, in which a positive role-model is provided by the heroine's Republican grandmother. Grandes's later fiction focuses on heterosexual relationships, sometimes but not always from a feminine perspective; the last, *The Frozen Heart* (*El corazón helado*, 2007), contributes to the vogue for novels about the Civil War.

Homosexualities

We have seen how several non-lesbian-identified women authors explore lesbian desire – others are Ana María Moix (1947–) with *Julia* (1969), and Esther Tusquets (1936–) with *The Same Sea Every Summer* (*El mismo mar todos los veranos*, 1978) and *Love is a Solitary Game* (*El amor es un juego solitario*, 1979). The lesbian poet Gloria Fuertes (1917–98), who published mostly under the Franco dictatorship, kept her sexual orientation separate from her writing. The most striking self-identified lesbian author has been Maria-Mercè Marçal (1952–98), writing in Catalan. Her novel *The Passion According to Renée Vivien* (*La passió segons Renée Vivien*, 1994), whose title evokes the Brazilian Clarice Lispector's *The Passion According to G.H.* (*A paixão segundo G.H.*), is a homage, in the modernist tradition of Virginia Woolf and Djuna Barnes, to the British-born French symbolist poet and open lesbian Pauline Tarn (pen-name Renée Vivien). Translator into Catalan of Colette, Yourcenar, Akhmatova, and Tsvetaeva, and feminist activist and theoretician, in her poetry Marçal draws on the popular Catalan song tradition to rework images of women. The poems of *Sister, Stranger* (*La germana, l'estrangera*, 1981–4) 'write the female body' to explore sameness and difference.

The first writers to openly depict male homosexuality were Antonio de Hoyos (1885–1940) and Álvaro Retana (1890–1970); both wrote hugely popular novellas for the cheap subscription series previously mentioned. Hoyos, publishing 1903–27, was an aristocratic dandy who flaunted homosexuality as a form of social dissidence, frequenting low-life haunts. His homoerotic fiction cultivates a morbid decadence. Retana, by contrast, flaunts a frivolous homoeroticism whose camp theatricality mirrors his involvement in cabaret as songwriter and costume- and set-designer. Most of his 60+ novellas were written 1917–22, for the same popular subscription series; while explicitly appealing to the homosexual reader, they were widely enjoyed for their guilt-free eroticism. Both Hoyos and Retana were after the Civil War imprisoned for having supported the Republic – Hoyos dying in jail, Retana being released in 1948.

From 1822 to 1928, sodomy was decriminalized in Spain (unlike England, France, and Italy). The 1870 Penal Code instituted sexual offences (indecent behaviour, corruption of minors, public scandal), without distinguishing between heterosexual and homosexual behaviour. The Primo de Rivera dictatorship's 1928 Penal Code created such a distinction, doubling the penalties for homosexuals; this was reversed by the Republic's 1932 decriminalization of homosexuality. The Republic's medically influenced 1933 Vagrancy and Delinquency Law introduced the concept of 'state of danger' (*estado peligroso*) to cover individuals 'at risk' of becoming delinquents, proposing preventive assistance. This concept was used by the Franco dictatorship to round up homosexuals who were seen as a threat despite having committed no crime. In 1954, the dictatorship amended the 1933 Law, prescribing internment of homosexuals in special labour camps. The 1970 Law of Social Danger and Rehabilitation changed this to internment in rehabilitation centres. In practice, throughout the dictatorship most arrested homosexuals were put in jail. The 1970 law was rescinded only in 1981, three years after the 1978 Democratic Constitution. In 2005, Spain legalized same-sex marriage.

The Primo de Rivera dictatorship's homophobic legislation of 1928 coincided with the high point of the Spanish avant-garde. Luis Cernuda (1902–63) moved to Madrid permanently in 1929, assuming his homosexuality as a Gidean ethical stance. His poetry defines identity in terms of desire rather than an inherent self, opting for the solitary pursuit of classical beauty, represented by the Helllenic male ideal. *Forbidden Pleasures* (*Los placeres prohibidos*, written 1931) is openly homoerotic, with its songs to sailors and beautiful adolescents. 'To a Dead Poet (F.G.L)' ('A un poeta muerto (F.G.L.)'), written on his friend Lorca's death, acknowledges Lorca's homosexuality at a time when it was not mentioned in public.

In 1929, Lorca's father fixed his trip to New York to snap him out of depression, caused by a homosexual relationship his father may not have known about. But the relationship was an open secret in Madrid, at a time of new anti-homosexual legislation. Lorca's father certainly did not know that at the time New York was nicknamed 'homosexual headquarters'; the main cruising area was Riverside Park just below Columbia University where Lorca resided. Lorca's year there coincided not only with the Harlem Renaissance but also with a vibrant homosexual cultural scene, closely linked to Harlem's sophisticated black playhouses, just north of Columbia University, whose revues Lorca frequented. Lorca's 1930 stay in Havana also introduced him to freer attitudes to homosexuality.

It would be a mistake to read homosexuality into everything Lorca wrote; suggestions that his tragedies of female infertility (*Yerma*, 1934) and female repression (*The House of Bernarda Alba*, 1936) are 'really' about his problems as a homosexual do not seem helpful. But the topic of homosexuality appears explicitly in his poetry and drama written in New York and Cuba or shortly after. It is hard to know what to make of his 'Ode to Walt Whitman' ('Oda a Walt Whitman') in *Poet in New York*, which rails against New York's 'fairies', listing the various Spanish and Cuban derogatory terms for effeminate homosexual, while praising Whitman's virile, classical love of male beauty. This is not a simple opposition since the poem exonerates 'the boy who dresses as a bride in the closet's darkness'. Lorca's highly experimental play *The Public (El público*, finished on his 1930 return to Spain) explores a range of sexual options, mostly homosexual, some of them tortured but not all, showing that homosexuality can mean many things. In this sense, Lorca's writing can be called 'queer' – the term used to refer to forms of homosexual desire that refuse fixed identity. The multiple layers of masks, beneath which are yet more masks, suggest a postmodern concept of identity as performance, with no stable core. The sexually ambiguous protagonist of his similarly surrealist drama *When Five Years Pass (Así que pasen cinco años*, written 1931) vacillates between his fiancée (who prefers the rugby player), the typist, and his male friends. Both plays contain a play-within-the-play, for that is all there is: theatre. Lorca's family authorized publication of *The Public* only in 1976 and of his homoerotic *Sonnets of Dark Love (Sonetos del amor oscuro*, written 1935–6) only in 1984.

Since the 1970s, a number of openly homosexual writers have cultivated popular fiction targeted at a gay readership, the best known being Eduardo Mendicutti (1948–). (I use the term 'gay' in the sense of a homosexual identity politics.) Terenci Moix, originally writing in Catalan, was a pioneer with his novel *The Day Marilyn Died (El dia que va morir Marilyn*, 1969): a homosexual *Bildungsroman*, whose contents are retraced in his later autobiography *El peso de la paja* (roughly translatable as *The Wanker's Burden*, 3 volumes, 1990–8). In the 1980s, he moved from a realist to a camp aesthetic, drawing on his lifelong passion for American cinema, epitomized in his Castilian-language romances set in Cleopatra's Egypt (courtesy of Hollywood); the first, *Don't Tell Me It Was a Dream (No digas que fue un sueño*, 1986), won Spain's biggest-paying Planeta Prize. Moix's ashes were scattered in Egypt's Valley of the Kings, at his request.

The contemporary poet and short-story writer Luis Antonio de Villena (1951–) has helped to reconstruct a Spanish homosexual literary tradition through his studies of Hoyos, Retana, and Cernuda among others. His own work combines an aestheticizing homoeroticism with high-cultural (often classical) references, exploring different kinds of marginalization. One of Spain's best, if uneven, contemporary authors is Álvaro Pombo (1939–), whose homosexual characters are explored through a philosophical investigation into appearance and substance. He has acknowledged his debt to Iris Murdoch from his years in England. His previously mentioned first book *Tales of Insubstantiality* depicts suburban London characters whose grey lives conceal unsuspected dramas. His work treats homosexuality in a matter-of-fact manner, yet it repeatedly precipitates tragedy. The banal, accidental nature of tragedy is explored in his masterly *The Iridized Platinum Rule* (*El metro de platino iridiado*, 1990), winner of the National Critics' Prize, in which the protagonist María's homosexual brother accidentally kills her son. At the end, María forms an unlikely alliance with the family's ageing camp friend; the two of them represent a transgendered caring for others that is compared to St Francis of Assisi.

As in Chapter 1, I close with Juan Goytisolo, as befits his importance. Read with hindsight, his pre-1966 realist fiction shows clear traces of the homosexuality he acknowledged in 1965. The fascination of Abel with the working-class Pablo in *Mourning in Paradise*, and of Pipo with the sailor Gorila in *Fiestas* (1958), mirrors Goytisolo's professed attraction, as son of a wealthy pro-Franco family, to proletarian men – illustrated also by the narrator-protagonist's relationship in *Marks of Identity* with the farmhand Jerónimo. His autobiography (see below) ends with his violent sexual encounter in Tangiers with a Moroccan dock worker, described as an 'ascesis' which, by purging his class guilt, frees him to write. In a similar scenario, the narrator of *Count Julian* – assuming the legendary persona of the traitor Count Julian who facilitated the 711 Arab invasion of Spain – corrupts and sodomizes Alvarito, his bourgeois boyhood self. As in the work of Genet – a decisive mentor for Goytisolo in Paris – betrayal is assumed as a way of transcending social stigmas by taking them on oneself.

Much of Goytisolo's writing inverts Francoist morality, adopting as a virtue everything it proscribed. This risks replicating Francoist ideology – implying, for example, that homosexuality is assumed because it is a perversion. The same logic governs the use of rape as a revolutionary tactic in *Count Julian*, whose latterday Arab invaders of Spain, fantasized through the lens of European orientalist fears, rape Spanish Christian womanhood. Liberation is equated with phallic aggression; worse, rape is depicted as liberating women sexually. In his lucid essays, Goytisolo disarms such criticism, insisting that he is not depicting real Arabs or Spaniards but using the ingredients of Francoist ideology to destroy it. The influence of Marcuse's equation of political and sexual repression is evident in his work from *Count Julian* on; he witnessed the May 1968 events in Paris.

Goytisolo's post-1966 novels replace plot and character with linguistic play, allowing a fluid concept of identity that breaks with his rigid Francoist upbringing. In *Virtues of the Solitary Bird* – whose title derives from St John of the Cross's lost work *The Properties of the Solitary Bird* (*Las propiedades del pájaro solitario*) – the liberation/violence equation is transmuted into a disturbing metaphorical association between mystical transcendence and AIDS. There is, however, no gender-bending: the fluid self is exclusively male – even the hermaphroditic Angel in *Makbara* (1980) confirms phallic power through his/her desire for the phallus. In his two-volume autobiography *Forbidden Zone* (*Coto vedado*, 1985) and *Realms of Strife* (*En los reinos de taifa*, 1986), Goytisolo has declared his attraction to virile, non-gay-identified men. Despite his public role as a critic of racism, he has dissociated himself from gay activism.

The aggression of much of Goytisolo's fiction is absent in his autobiography – perhaps the most lucid and self-reflexive memoir

16. Juan Goytisolo and Monique Lange, 1964

in the Spanish language. It is an explicit confession narrative.
His frank account of his childhood – his mother's death in a
Nationalist air raid in the Civil War (which did not alter the
family's pro-Franco stance), sexual molestation by his grandfather
– is matched by that of his clumsy journey towards coming out. The
text includes the moving 1965 letter in which he 'confessed' his
homosexuality to his life-long partner Monique Lange, whom he
married in 1978. Contrasting with his novels' phallic stance, his
autobiography pays tribute to the women in his life: Monique and
her daughter, and female servants in Barcelona and Paris. The
'rebirth' depicted at its end coincides with the death of the nanny
who brought him up as a substitute mother. The autobiography
oscillates between a tendency to contrast a false self, imposed by
his upbringing, with a gradually discovered authentic self, and
awareness that all identities are constructed. It closes by
recognizing that writing can only create fictions.

Chapter 4
Cultural patrimony

This final chapter considers two aspects of cultural patrimony: who has access to it, and how it is transmitted to future generations. Both raise issues about the ownership of culture. I discuss just a few examples.

Taking culture to the people

The Spanish Republic of 1931–9 was a major experiment in broadening access to culture. Its governments (excepting the conservative interlude of 1933 to early 1936) brought together left-liberals, socialists and communists. Spain's strong anarchist movement, rejecting all state control, boycotted the Republic in peace-time but supported it during the Civil War to help defeat the Nationalist military insurrection. Nationalist victory on 1 April 1939 was a major cultural as well as political setback, with the exodus of the huge majority of Spain's intellectuals and teachers, who supported the Republic because of its prioritization of education. Those pro-Republican intellectuals and teachers that stayed, if they escaped execution or imprisonment, were 'purged' and denied work.

Although the various pro-Republican groups had political differences, they all believed that culture was the key to

17. Girl reading a book from a village library created by the Pedagogical Missions, 1932

incorporating the lower classes into a democratic society. Urban workers had since the early 20th century had access to socialist or anarchist cultural centres (Casas del Pueblo), but the rural masses had little schooling. The Republic's cultural programme does, however, show tension between a desire to take bourgeois culture to the masses and a more radical attempt to redefine culture in non-bourgeois terms.

In 1931, Spain's illiteracy rate was 40%, much higher in rural areas. The Republic created over 2,000 schools a year, stocked with libraries for adult use as well. An additional 5,000 libraries were created in small villages by the Pedagogical Missions (Misiones Pedagógicas) founded in 1931 to take culture to remote rural areas; they additionally toured villages with mobile 'book buses' (*bibliobuses*). By 1933, when the incoming conservative government cut back the Missions' budget, these small village libraries had been used by nearly 300,000 children and 200,000 adults. The Missions were staffed by student volunteers; for the young women who participated, it was an unprecedented emancipatory experience. The Pedagogical Missions also taught literacy skills and toured villages with reproductions of artworks, recorded music, films, and live theatre. Their People's Theatre (Teatro del Pueblo) was directed by the playwright Alejandro Casona (1903–65), with amateur student actors. More attention has been given to the smaller travelling student theatre company, La Barraca, also funded by the Republican Government, since its director was Lorca. Lorca spoke enthusiastically about La Barraca's untutored peasant audiences, since, having no experience of bourgeois realism but versed in popular carnival and street festivals, they appreciated his productions as spectacle, in keeping with his avant-garde aims. ('*Barraca*' means 'fairground booth'.)

This return to the primitive roots of theatre was decisive for Lorca's career: in the 1930s, he devoted himself exclusively to the stage. To see his 1930s rural tragedies as a return to realism is

18. Federico García Lorca, wearing the blue overalls donned by Republican activists, with a poster for his travelling theatre company La Barraca

to ignore his experiences with rural audiences. Both La Barraca and the People's Theatre focused on the classics of Golden Age theatre, to give the unlettered access to the nation's cultural patrimony. But these were experimental productions, with stylized modern sets – minimalist because the stage apparatus had to be packed into a lorry. The brief surviving film footage of Lorca acting the role of Death in Calderón's morality play *Life is a Dream* shows costumes verging on the surrealist. That Lorca chose to stage this religious play shows his awareness of building on popular familiarity with religious ritual. Other plays were chosen because they illustrated the Republic's democratizing agenda: La Barraca's production of Lope de Vega's *Fuenteovejuna*, in which the peasants assume collective responsibility for executing their abusive Governor, omitted the last scene in which the Catholic Monarchs approve the peasants' behaviour. Lorca's decision to cut this ending turned the play into an endorsement of popular revolution, producing a furore in the conservative press.

The Pedagogical Missions' activities were extensively documented: the photographs focus mainly on the peasant audiences, capturing their rapture on first exposure to theatre, movies, paintings and classical music. These photos demonstrate culture's role in constructing community, but they also depict the villagers as an audience receiving a cultural heritage brought from the city. Once the Civil War broke out, the Republic's cultural effort – which, extraordinarily, intensified in wartime – became more geared to giving agency to the peasantry, who formed the bulk of the Republican troops. The government department People's Culture (Cultura Popular) created libraries at the front, and in hospitals, kindergartens, and workers' centres.

Literacy Flying Brigades (Brigadas Volantes de Lucha contra el Analfabetismo) took literacy to an estimated 70,000 soldiers in the trenches and around 300,000 adults on the home front. A number of theatre groups toured the war front, to raise soldiers' morale, or performed urban street theatre to recruit troops. The

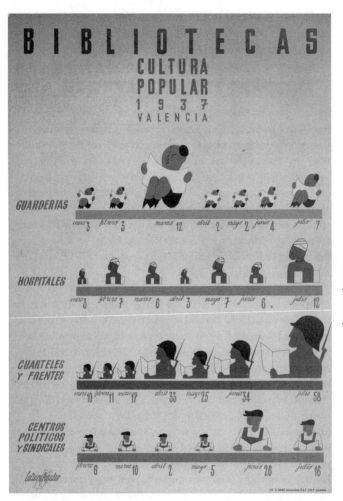

19. Republican Spanish Civil War poster issued by People's Culture, giving statistics for new libraries created during the war, 1937

author of a prewar *proletcult* drama, *Dock Strike* (*Huelga en el puerto*, 1933), María Teresa León directed the Madrid-based Art and Propaganda Theatre (Teatro de Arte y Propaganda) and, from early 1938, the Theatre Guerrillas (Guerrillas del Teatro) which performed at the front. Among the dramatists contributing *agitprop* theatre was her husband Rafael Alberti, whose brilliantly inventive *Radio Seville* (*Radio Sevilla*, 1938) draws on a burlesque music-hall tradition. In 1936, León and Alberti founded the Communist-backed cultural magazine *Blue Overalls* (*El Mono Azul*) to support the war effort; León served as Secretary of the international Communist Antifascist Writers' Alliance (Alianza de Escritores Antifascistas). The other major wartime cultural magazine was the left-liberal *Spain's Hour* (*Hora de España*), whose most frequent contributor was the poet Antonio Machado (1875–1939). Machado's grave at Colliure, where he died crossing the border to France, is a pilgrimage site still today.

The Spanish Civil War has been called the 'Poets' War' because of the number of poets (Spanish and foreign) who participated in the Republic's war effort. Manuel Altolaguirre (1905–59) directed a re-vamped wartime La Barraca and ran a frontline printing press. The former child goatherd, Miguel Hernández (1910–42), ran a propaganda unit and wrote agitprop theatre and poetry, assuming the role of collective poetic voice in *Wind of the People* (*Viento del pueblo*, 1937). The Republican Government published poetry anthologies, privileging collective over individual expression. But the most remarkable wartime cultural production was the mass of poetry written by ordinary soldiers or civilians, many of them recently introduced to literacy by the Republic's literacy campaigns, who were encouraged to send poems to magazines run by trade unions and political organizations, or to the regular column *Ballad Book of the War* (*Romancero de la guerra*) published in *Blue Overalls* till May 1937. Soldiers were also encouraged to pin their poems on newsboards (*murales*) at the front, which functioned as a collective grassroots chronicle of the war. Some 1,376 Republican wartime magazines publishing poetry have been counted, and some 8,500 poems survive, mostly signed but by unknown individuals, a few by women and children. This massive poetic production allowed soldiers and civilians to 'write the war'. War poems by established poets sometimes use avant-garde verse forms, but the vast majority of this poetic output – by established and amateur poets alike – adopts the popular ballad form (*romance*) familiar to the unlettered. The ballad form allowed recital at the front, often with guitar accompaniment, continuing for emancipatory purposes an oral tradition unbroken since the Middle Ages. The ballad's regular rhythms made this poetry 'memorable'. Although most poems were signed, their insertion into a popular oral tradition broke with a high-cultural concept of poetry as an elite literary genre, and with the bourgeois concept of the writer as individual genius.

Writers and the heritage industry

The Spanish Republic's cultural programme is unparalleled. By contrast, the vibrancy of a cultural heritage industry in Spain today indicates the country's immersion in the global marketplace, which turns the past into a commodity. The use of literature to promote cultural heritage is not new: Berceo's mid-13th-century *Life of St Emilian* (*Vida de San Millán*) and *Miracles of Our Lady* (*Milagros de Nuestra Señora*), the oldest Spanish literary works by a named writer, were written to boost local cults at the monastery of San Millán de la Cogolla in La Rioja, near the pilgrimage route to Santiago de Compostela. The *Poem of the Cid* (late 12th century?) was used in the late 13th century to promote tomb cults at the monastery of San Pedro de Cardeña, near Burgos, where the Cid and his wife (and allegedly his horse) were buried. What is specific to the modern period is the promotion of literature itself as a form of cultural heritage. The culture of commemoration started in Spain in the late 19th century with the erection of monuments to national figures (including writers) and the celebration of anniversaries of national events. The first major anniversary celebration of a writer was the 1905 tercentenary of *Don Quixote* Part I, for which Unamuno and Azorín wrote their essays on Don Quixote (see Introduction). Chapter 2 noted the importance for the 1920s poetic avant-garde of the 1927 tercentenary of Góngora's death. This culture of commemoration has intensified in the 21st century, with the creation in 2002 of the State Society for Cultural Commemorations (Sociedad Estatal de Conmemoraciones Culturales).

The biggest literary commemoration to date was the 400-year anniversary of *Don Quixote* Part I in 2005. The Ministry of Culture invited bids for state funding totalling 30 million euros. Guests

20. Two-euro coin minted for the 2005 fourth centenary commemoration of the first edition of *Don Quixote*, Part I

at Spain's state-owned Paradores (chain of heritage hotels) found a modernized, abridged version of the *Quixote* in their bedrooms. The autonomous government of Castilla-La Mancha set up a limited company 'Don Quixote 2005, Inc.' ('Don Quijote de la Mancha 2005, S.A.'). Companies granted permission to use the Quijote IV Centenario's official logo in their advertising included department stores, travel agents, and manufacturers of cars, beer, food products, detergent and cosmetics. 'Don Quixote 2005, Inc.' organized a 'Quijote Rock' concert, and Spain's National Library held a rap session based on Cervantes's text ('Quijote Hip Hop') with break-dancers, graffiti artists and disc jockeys. These appeals to youth raised eyebrows but, as seen in the Introduction, the *Quixote* has been re-read constantly over the centuries (its start was recently translated into Spanglish). However, the saturation of Spanish supermarkets throughout 2005 with stands selling the *Quixote* served only to produce *Quixote* fatigue, as did the 1,400 *Quixote*-related events organized by Spain's state agency for promoting Spanish language and culture abroad, predictably titled the Cervantes Institute (Instituto Cervantes, created 1991).

The problem here is state patronage, which can kill cultural heritage by turning it into a patriotic duty – what the theorist of collective memory, Pierre Nora, has called *devoir de mémoire* (obligation to remember). Much more effective are the large number of writers' house-museums, mostly set up by local governments seeking cultural rather than financial capital. These are small-scale, intimate affairs, with the added value of authentic settings lived in by the author – though in some cases the period furniture is not the author's own. Many have displays of the writer's work, as well as biographical documentation. The national Association of House-Museums (ACAMFE) lists 52 museums located in writers' former homes; this excludes house-museums which are not ACAMFE members (such as those in Catalonia or those run by the central state). One of the oldest writer's house-museums in Spain is that devoted to Galdós in Las Palmas de Gran Canaria, whose library contains many of his manuscripts.

21. Galdós's cradle displayed in his house-museum at Las Palmas de Gran Canaria

In fact, Galdós left the Canaries to study in Madrid and returned only once, late in his career; the museum displays his cradle, to establish the building's credentials as his birthplace. The substantial authentic displays come from Galdós's summer home in Santander: the Santander Municipal Government refused his daughter's request that the villa be turned into a museum, since Galdós was known as an anticlerical liberal. She therefore sold the villa's contents to the Gran Canaria island government in 1959. When the museum opened in 1964, the Bishop of Las Palmas threatened to excommunicate anyone who visited it.

Political controversy also dogs the estate of Galdós' fellow realist novelist, Emilia Pardo Bazán. Her Galician country home, the Pazos de Meirás, was 'donated' to General Franco by 'the people of Galicia' at the end of Civil War. Effectively, Pardo Bazán's sole surviving daughter was obliged to sell it below market value to the Nationalist Provincial Governor, the money being raised through extortion, including local employers docking a day's pay from workers. Franco's family still lives there, and to date has not allowed access to verify what is left of Pardo Bazán's library; much of it is rumoured to have been burnt or sold. In June 2009, the Galician Autonomous Government won a protracted lawsuit against Franco's daughter, declaring the building a listed site, which requires public access to be granted on four days a month; this has not yet been implemented. Attempts to claim the property for Galicia on the grounds that it was purchased under duress have so far failed. The Galician Royal Academy (Real Academia Galega) is housed in Pardo Bazán's townhouse in Corunna, whose middle floor is her house-museum. The RAG's library upstairs contains her substantial Corunna library. The house-museum's contents are Pardo Bazán's own, and the museum's director has given the documentary section a refreshing feminist emphasis. The most visited Galician house-museum is that of Rosalía de Castro in Padrón, opened in 1972 in the house where she died. A shrine to Galician nationalism, it is filled with tributes from Galician emigrant communities in the Americas.

Cervantes has two house-museums. The most intimate is the state-owned Museo Casa de Cervantes in Valladolid: the house where he lived from 1604 to 1606, when Part I of the *Quixote* was completed. The house was bought for the state in 1912 thanks partly to the American millionaire Archer Huntington, founder of the Hispanic Society of America in New York. Foreign involvement in Spain's cultural patrimony is a sensitive issue: Huntington's early 20th-century purchase of a magnificent collection of Spanish first editions and manuscripts raised the hackles of Spain's major literary historian and National Library Director, Marcelino Menéndez y Pelayo (1856–1912). Many bibliographic treasures have been lost to the nation through pillage, particularly with the sacking of libraries by Napoleon's troops during the 1808–14 French occupation. Countless medieval manuscripts were also lost thanks to the Spanish liberal state's mid-19th-century disentailments, which nationalized Church property, selling off

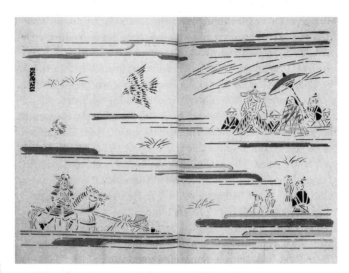

22. Illustration from a 1936 Japanese edition of *Don Quixote*, representing him as a samurai warrior, displayed at the Museo Casa Natal de Cervantes

monasteries and their priceless libraries to private bidders. The Right has persistently contested the Republic's sequestering of private libraries during the Civil War, to put them in safe storage; after the war, the Franco dictatorship did not, however, return these libraries to their owners but put them in the National Library – although unjust, this made them available to the nation.

Cervantes' other museum is the house where he was born in Alcalá de Henares (Museo Casa Natal de Cervantes), owned by the Madrid autonomous government. Close to Madrid, it is a major tourist draw. The rooms (with period furniture unrelated to Cervantes) are cordoned off, with somewhat alienating soundscapes of 'voices from the time'. But the museum does house a wonderful collection of Spanish and foreign editions of Cervantes' work, many of them displayed. In the tourist season, the 'Cervantes Train' runs between Madrid and Alcalá, offering

'Cervantine entertainment'. There are now multiple 'literary routes' advertised on the Internet, including the 'Route of the Cid', 'Cervantes Route' and 'Lorca Route'. There are even tours of Madrid sites mentioned in Pérez-Reverte's Alatriste historical novels, and of the Barcelona that appears in Ruiz Zafón's bestseller *The Shadow of the Wind*. A very different use of heritage is Goytisolo's work to get Marrakesh's Xemaá-el-Fná marketplace – whose oral storytellers and carnivalesque confusion of bodies end his novel *Makbara* – saved from urban development. His campaign helped to create UNESCO's Intangible Heritage programme in 1997, with Xemaá-el-Fná among the first listed sites. While the UNESCO heritage site label will increase tourism, it preserves the marketplace for the local people who use it.

Although the heritage industry is a form of commercialization, when done well it introduces a broad public to writers who might otherwise be read only by scholars. Most of the Spanish visitors at the house-museums I toured were families with young children; practically all these museums have publications and workshops for children. Particularly imaginative are the activities at Lorca's house-museum at the Huerta de San Vicente in Granada, led by actors who use Lorca's work to encourage children to write their own poetry. The Huerta de San Vicente is filled with furnishings, paintings and photographs donated by Lorca's family, including his piano (he was an accomplished pianist), used for concerts. The paintings and photographs give an insight into his cultural networks. Lorca's second house-museum at Fuentevaqueros – much visited since he was born there – has an exhibition space (which shows the surviving footage of La Barraca) and is developing a study centre, to which Lorca's biographer Ian Gibson has donated his papers. The third Lorca museum in the village of Valderrubio, the family's summer home, has no works by Lorca but has adopted an ethnographic approach, recreating the atmosphere of a working village house in Lorca's time. The furnishings were donated by villagers to whom the Lorca family had given them away, or are gifts from local families who knew

Lorca when he lived there as a child or came back for the summers. The guide, a neighbour, has an inexhaustible knowledge of village lore. The result is a sense of communal investment in the museum. The view of the Sierra Nevada from Lorca's bedroom is stunning. Of all the house-museums I visited to write this chapter, this was the one that gave me a sense of what it might have been like for the writer concerned to live there.

What we really want from house-museums is, after all, the writer rather than the work. The objects in house-museums are much like relics that stand for the writer's absent body. One of the reasons that the 'pilgrimage' to Lorca's house-museums is so poignant is that no one knows where his body is: his house-museums serve as a substitute. When in December 2009, against his family's wishes, the Andalusian autonomous government ordered excavation of the site outside Alfácar (Granada) where he was allegedly buried after execution, no human remains were found. The longstanding dispute over whether his supposed grave should be opened raised major issues about the ownership of writers' bodies. Cervantes' body has also disappeared, with the rebuilding later in the 17th century of the Madrid convent (San Ildefonso de Trinitarias Descalzas) where he was buried in 1616. Although we say that writers live on in their works, in practice they do not, since – as Borges' story 'Pierre Menard' demonstrates – we can never get back to the original meaning that a literary work had for its author. Given this impossibility, the material evidence of an author's existence provided by house-museums has a compensatory magic. There is all the difference in the world between the closet in Rosalía de Castro's house-museum, filled with period clothes that are not hers, and the closet in Galdós's house-museum, which contains the jacket, waistcoat, shirts, and boots he wore himself. By contrast with the material possessions of past writers displayed in house-museums, their works live on, not as authentic expressions of their author, but in our interpretations of them.

Further reading

The following list details some of the best studies in English. It also serves as partial acknowledgement of my English-language sources.

Historical studies

R. Carr (ed.), *Spain: A History* (Oxford University Press, 2000); B. F. Reilly, *The Medieval Spains* (Cambridge University Press, 1993); J. H. Elliott, *Imperial Spain* (Penguin, 2002); R. Carr, *Spain, 1808–1975* (Oxford University Press, 1982); A. Shubert, *A Social History of Modern Spain* (Routledge, 1990); H. Graham and J. Labanyi (eds.), *Spanish Cultural Studies: An Introduction* (Oxford University Press, 1995). See also: H. Kamen, *The Disinherited: Exile and the Making of Spanish Culture, 1492–1975* (Harper, 2007).

Works covering more than one period

D. T. Gies (ed.), *The Cambridge History of Spanish Literature* (Cambridge University Press, 2004) provides a detailed, authoritative survey. See also G. Dopico Black, *Medieval and Early Modern Spanish Literature*; and L. E. Delgado and J. Labanyi, *Modern Spanish Literature*, both in the Cultural History of Literature series (Polity, forthcoming).

On non-Castilian literatures: K. Hooper and M. Puga Moruxa (eds.), *Contemporary Galician Cultural Studies* (Modern Language Association of America, 2010); W. A. Douglass (ed.), *Basque Cultural Studies* (University of Nevada Press, 2000); A. Terry, *A Companion*

to Catalan Literature (Tamesis, 2003). For Catalan literature, see
also the excellent Catalan–Spanish–English website www.lletra.net
(accessed 9 April 2010) of the Catalan Open University (Universitat
Oberta de Catalunya).

On gender issues: L. Vollendorf (ed.), *Recovering Spain's Feminist
Tradition* (Modern Language Association of America, 2001); P. J. Smith,
*The Body Hispanic: Gender and Sexuality in Spanish and Spanish
American Literature* (Oxford University Press, 1989); C. Davies,
Spanish Women's Writing 1849–1996 (Athlone Press, 1998); J. C. Wilcox,
Women Poets of Spain, 1860–1990 (University of Illinois Press, 1997).

Medieval literature

On Muslim and Jewish culture: J. D. Dodds, M. R. Menocal, and
A. K. Balbale, *The Arts of Intimacy: Christians, Jews, and Muslims
in the Making of Castilian Culture* (Yale University Press, 2008);
M. M. Hamilton, S. J. Portnoy, and D. Wacks (eds.), *Wine, Women and
Song: Hebrew and Arabic Literature of Medieval Iberia* (Juan de la
Cuesta, 2004); M. R. Menocal, *The Ornament of the World: How
Muslims, Jews, and Christians Created a Culture of Tolerance in
Medieval Spain* (Little, Brown & Co., 2002); M. R. Menocal,
R. P. Scheindlin, and M. Selis (eds.), *The Literature of al-Andalus*,
in the Cambridge History of Arabic Literature series (Cambridge
University Press, 2000).

See also: J. Blackmore and G. S. Hutcheson (eds.), *Queer Iberia:
Sexualities, Cultures, and Crossings from the Middle Ages to the
Renaissance* (Duke University Press, 1999); E. M. Gerli and J. Weiss
(eds.), *Poetry at Court in Trastamaran Spain* (Arizona State University
Press, 1998); S. Gilman, *The Spain of Fernando de Rojas: The
Intellectual and Social Landscape of 'La Celestina'* (Princeton
University Press, 1972); R. González Echevarría, *Celestina's Brood*
(Duke University Press, 1993); L. M. Haywood and L. O. Vasvári (eds.),
A Companion to the 'Libro de Buen Amor' (Tamesis, 2004); O. Martín
and S. Pinet (eds.), 'Theories of Medieval Iberia', Special Issue of
Diacritics 36 (2006): 3–4; C. Smith, *The Making of the 'Poema de mio
Cid'* (Cambridge University Press, 1983); J. Weiss, *The 'Mester de
Clerecía': Intellectuals and Ideologues in 13th-Century Castile*
(Tamesis, 2006).

Early modern literature

On Cervantes: A. J. Cascardi (ed.), *The Cambridge Companion to Cervantes* (Cambridge University Press, 2002); W. Childers, *Transnational Cervantes* (University of Toronto Press, 2006); A. Close, *The Romantic Approach to 'Don Quixote'* (Cambridge University Press, 1977); A. J. Cruz and C. B. Johnson (eds.), *Cervantes and His Postmodern Constituencies* (Garland, 1999); B. Fuchs, *Passing for Spain: Cervantes and the Fictions of Identity* (University of Illinois Press, 2003); R. González Echevarría, *Cervantes' 'Don Quixote': A Casebook* (Oxford University Press, 2005), and *Love and the Law in Cervantes* (Yale University Press, 2005).

On gender issues: M. S. Brownlee, *The Cultural Labyrinth of María de Zayas* (University of Pennsylvania Press, 2000); G. Dopico Black, *Perfect Wives, Other Women: Adultery and Inquisition in Early Modern Spain* (Duke University Press, 2001); M. McKendrick, *Woman and Society in the Spanish Drama of the Golden Age* (Cambridge University Press, 1974); S. Velasco, *The Lieutenant Nun: Transgenderism, Lesbian Desire, and Catalina de Erauso* (University of Texas Press, 2000); A. Weber, *Teresa of Avila and the Rhetoric of Femininity* (Princeton University Press, 1996).

See also: M. S. Brownlee and U. Gumbrecht (eds.), *Cultural Authority in Golden Age Spain* (Johns Hopkins University Press, 1995); A. J. Cruz, *Discourses of Poverty: Social Reform and the Picaresque Novel in Early Modern Spain* (University of Toronto Press, 1999); B. Fuchs, *Exotic Nation: Maurophilia and the Construction of Early Modern Spain* (University of Pennsylvania Press, 2009); R. Greene, *Unrequited Conquests: Love and Empire in the Colonial Americas* (University of Chicago Press, 1999); J. Robbins, *The Challenges of Uncertainty: An Introduction to 17th-Century Spanish Literature* (Rowman & Littlefield, 1998).

18th- and 19th-century literature

On gender issues: L. Charnon-Deutsch, *Narratives of Desire: 19th-Century Spanish Fiction by Women* (Pennsylvania State University Press, 1994); L. Charnon-Deutsch and J. Labanyi (eds.), *Culture and Gender in 19th-Century Spain* (Oxford University Press,

1995); R. Haidt, *Embodying Enlightenment: Knowing the Body in 18th-Century Spanish Literature and Culture* (Palgrave Macmillan, 1998); C. Jagoe, *Ambiguous Angels: Gender in the Novels of Galdós* (University of California Press, 1994); S. Kirkpatrick, *Las Románticas: Women Writers and Subjectivity in Spain, 1835–1850* (University of California Press, 1989); J. Labanyi, *Gender and Modernization in the Spanish Realist Novel* (Oxford University Press, 2000); A. Sinclair, *Dislocations of Desire: Gender, Identity, and Strategy in 'La Regenta'* (University of North Carolina Press, 1998).

On Galdós: T. Fuentes Peris, *Visions of Filth: Deviancy and Social Control in the Novels of Galdós* (Liverpool University Press, 2003); H. Gold, *The Reframing of Realism: Galdós and the Discourses of the 19th-Century Spanish Novel* (Duke University Press, 1993); J. Labanyi (ed.), *Galdós* (Longman, 1993); G. Ribbans, *History and Fiction in Galdós's Narratives* (Oxford University Press, 1993).

See also: M. Iarocci, *Properties of Modernity: Romantic Spain, Modern Europe, and the Legacies of Empire* (Vanderbilt University Press, 2006); W. C. Ríos Font, *The Canon and the Archive: Configuring Literature in Modern Spain* (Bucknell University Press, 2004).

20th- and 21st-century literature

Useful surveys: D. T. Gies (ed.), *The Cambridge Companion to Modern Spanish Literature* (Cambridge University Press, 1999); C. Perriam, M. Thompson, S. Frenk, and V. Knights, *A New History of Spanish Writing, 1939 to the 1990s* (Oxford University Press, 2000).

On gender issues: E. L. Bergmann and R. Herr (eds.), *Mirrors and Echoes: Women's Writing in Contemporary Spain* (University of California Press, 2007); B. S. Epps, Significant Violence: *Oppression and Resistance in the Narratives of Juan Goytisolo, 1970–1990* (Oxford University Press, 1996); O. Ferrán and K. M. Glenn (eds.), *Women's Narrative and Film in 20th-Century Spain* (Routledge, 2002); C. Henseler, *Contemporary Spanish Women's Narrative and the Publishing Industry* (University of Illinois Press, 2003); R. Johnson, *Gender and Nation in the Spanish Modernist Novel* (Vanderbilt University Press, 2003); E. Scarlett, *Under Construction: The Body in Spanish Novels* (University Press of Virginia, 1994);

P. J. Smith, *Laws of Desire: Questions of Homosexuality in Spanish Literature and Film*, 1960–80 (Clarendon Press, 1992).

On Lorca: M. M. Delgado, *Federico García Lorca* (Routledge, 2008); P. J. Smith, *The Theatre of García Lorca: Text, Performance, Psychoanalysis* (Cambridge University Press, 1998).

On Republican exiles: S. Faber, *Exile and Cultural Hegemony: Spanish Intellectuals in Mexico, 1939–1975* (Vanderbilt University Press, 2002); H. López and M. P. Balibrea (eds.), 'Rethinking Spanish Republican Exile', Special Issue of *Journal of Spanish Cultural Studies*, 6.1 (2005).

See also: M. M. Delgado, *'Other' Spanish Theatres* (Manchester University Press, 2003); C. Henseler and R. D. Pope (eds.), *Generation X Rocks: Contemporary Spanish Fiction, Film, and Rock Culture* (Vanderbilt University Press, 2007); J. Labanyi, *Myth and History in the Contemporary Spanish Novel* (Cambridge University Press, 1986); A. Loureiro, *The Ethics of Autobiography: Replacing the Subject in Modern Spain* (Vanderbilt University Press, 2000); J. Mayhew, *The Twilight of the Avant-Garde: Spanish Poetry 1980–2000* (Liverpool University Press, 2009); D. L. Parsons, *A Cultural History of Madrid: Modernism and the Urban Spectacle* (Berg, 2003); A. Sinclair, *Trafficking Knowledge in 20th-Century Spain: Centres of Exchange and Cultural Imaginaries* (Tamesis, 2009), and *Uncovering the Mind: Unamuno, the Unknown and the Vicissitudes of the Self* (Manchester University Press, 2002); S. Wright, *Tales of Seduction: The Figure of Don Juan in Spanish Culture* (Tauris Academic Studies, 2007).

Index

Index

Index

CLASSICS
A Very Short Introduction
Mary Beard and John Henderson

This Very Short Introduction to Classics links a haunting temple on a lonely mountainside to the glory of ancient Greece and the grandeur of Rome, and to Classics within modern culture – from Jefferson and Byron to Asterix and Ben-Hur.

'The authors show us that Classics is a "modern" and sexy subject. They succeed brilliantly in this regard … nobody could fail to be informed and entertained – and the accent of the book is provocative and stimulating.'

John Godwin, _Times Literary Supplement_

'Statues and slavery, temples and tragedies, museum, marbles, and mythology – this provocative guide to the Classics demystifies its varied subject-matter while seducing the reader with the obvious enthusiasm and pleasure which mark its writing.'

Edith Hall

MUSIC
A Very Short Introduction
Nicholas Cook

This stimulating Very Short Introduction to music
invites us to really *think* about music and the values
and qualities we ascribe to it.

> 'A *tour de force*. Nicholas Cook is without doubt one of
> the most probing and creative thinkers about music we
> have today.'
>
> **Jim Samson, University of Bristol**

> 'Nicholas Cook offers a perspective that is clearly influ-
> enced by recent writing in a host of disciplines related
> to music. It may well prove a landmark in the appreci-
> ation of the topic ... In short, I can hardly imagine it being
> done better.'
>
> **Roger Parker, University of Cambridge**

PSYCHOLOGY
A Very Short Introduction
Gillian Butler and Freda McManus

Psychology: A Very Short Introduction provides an up-to-date overview of the main areas of psychology, translating complex psychological matters, such as perception, into readable topics so as to make psychology accessible for newcomers to the subject. The authors use everyday examples as well as research findings to foster curiosity about how and why the mind works in the way it does, and why we behave in the ways we do. This book explains why knowing about psychology is important and relevant to the modern world.

'a very readable, stimulating, and well-written introduction to psychology which combines factual information with a welcome honesty about the current limits of knowledge. It brings alive the fascination and appeal of psychology, its significance and implications, and its inherent challenges.'

Anthony Clare

'This excellent text provides a succinct account of how modern psychologists approach the study of the mind and human behaviour. ... the best available introduction to the subject.'

Anthony Storr

www.oup.co.uk/vsi/psychology

POLITICS
A Very Short Introduction
Kenneth Minogue

In this provocative but balanced essay, Kenneth Minogue discusses the development of politics from the ancient world to the twentieth century. He prompts us to consider why political systems evolve, how politics offers both power and order in our society, whether democracy is always a good thing, and what future politics may have in the twenty-first century.

> 'This is a fascinating book which sketches, in a very short space, one view of the nature of politics ... the reader is challenged, provoked and stimulated by Minogue's trenchant views.'
>
> **Ian Davies, *Talking Politics***

> 'a dazzling but unpretentious display of great scholarship and humane reflection'
>
> **Neil O'Sullivan, University of Hull**

www.oup.co.uk/vsi/politics

ARCHAEOLOGY
A Very Short Introduction
Paul Bahn

This entertaining Very Short Introduction reflects the enduring popularity of archaeology – a subject which appeals as a pastime, career, and academic discipline, encompasses the whole globe, and surveys 2.5 million years. From deserts to jungles, from deep caves to mountain tops, from pebble tools to satellite photographs, from excavation to abstract theory, archaeology interacts with nearly every other discipline in its attempts to reconstruct the past.

'very lively indeed and remarkably perceptive … a quite brilliant and level-headed look at the curious world of archaeology'
Barry Cunliffe, University of Oxford

'It is often said that well-written books are rare in archaeology, but this is a model of good writing for a general audience. The book is full of jokes, but its serious message – that archaeology can be a rich and fascinating subject – it gets across with more panache than any other book I know.'
Simon Denison, editor of *British Archaeology*

www.oup.co.uk/vsi/archaeology

SOCIOLOGY
A Very Short Introduction
Steve Bruce

Drawing on studies of social class, crime and deviance, work in bureaucracies, and changes in religious and political organizations, this Very Short Introduction explores the tension between the individual's role in society and society's role in shaping the individual, and demonstrates the value of sociology as a perspective for understanding the modern world.

'Steve Bruce has made an excellent job of a difficult task, one which few practising sociologists could have accomplished with such aplomb. The arguments are provocatively and intelligently presented, and the tone and the style are also laudable.'

Gordon Marshall, University of Oxford

www.oup.co.uk/vsi/sociology

THEOLOGY
A Very Short Introduction
David F. Ford

This Very Short Introduction provides both believers and non-believers with a balanced survey of the central questions of contemporary theology. David Ford's interrogative approach draws the reader into considering the principles underlying religious belief, including the centrality of salvation to most major religions, the concept of God in ancient, modern, and post-modern contexts, the challenge posed to theology by prayer and worship, and the issue of sin and evil. He also probes the nature of experience, knowledge, and wisdom in theology, and discusses what is involved in interpreting theological texts today.

'David Ford tempts his readers into the huge resources of theology with an attractive mix of simple questions and profound reflection. With its vivid untechnical language it succeeds brilliantly in its task of introduction.'
Stephen Sykes, University of Durham

'a fine book, imaginatively conceived and gracefully written. It carries the reader along with it, enlarging horizons while acknowledging problems and providing practical guidance along the way.'
Maurice Wiles, University of Oxford

www.oup.co.uk/vsi/theology